ALL YOU NEED TO KNOW ABOUT

BLOCKCHAIN CRYPTOCURRENCY AND NFTs

AMEY VARTAK

© **Amey Vartak 2023**

All rights reserved

All rights reserved by author. No part of this publication may be reproduced, stored in a retrieval system or transmitted in any form or by any means, electronic, mechanical, photocopying, recording or otherwise, without the prior permission of the author.

Although every precaution has been taken to verify the accuracy of the information contained herein, the author and publisher assume no responsibility for any errors or omissions. No liability is assumed for damages that may result from the use of information contained within.

First Published in January 2023

ISBN: 978-93-5628-172-1

BLUEROSE PUBLISHERS

www.BlueRoseONE.com

info@bluerosepublishers.com

+91 8882 898 898

Cover Design:

Yash

Typographic Design:

Tanya Raj Upadhyay

Distributed by: BlueRose, Amazon, Flipkart

Dedicated to my grand parents

Aaji & Azoba

Amey is a multi-talented human with over 10+ years of experience in software industry.

He can be also called as product designer, enterprise solutions designer, developer, consultant, mentor or by any other market defined function-title.

Fueled by high energy levels and boundless enthusiasm, Amey inspires his team members, clients & students he mentors.

He is MVP (Most Valuable Professional) and a certified Microsoft Solution Architect Expert.

Abundant energy fuels him to pursuit many other interests & hobbies. He has scored in 5 National Level Sports & has a Black Belt in Kick Boxing.

He can be reach on hello@ameyvartak.com & Insta : ameyvartakdev

Let's Build Something Great Together….

TABLE OF CONTENTS

INTRODUCTION

You may have heard the term "blockchain" thrown around a lot lately, but what does it mean? Cryptocurrency is also becoming more and more popular, but what is it? And what are NFTs?

To stay ahead of the curve in today's digital world, you must understand the technologies underlying cryptocurrencies and decentralized applications. This book will explore blockchain technology, cryptocurrency, and non-fungible tokens (NFTs). We will discuss how these technologies work and why they are so important. By the end of this book, you will have a solid understanding of these revolutionary technologies and be ready to join the revolution!

This book will provide you with an essential guide to understanding these technologies. You will learn about blockchain technology, how cryptocurrencies work, and Non-Fungible Tokens. We will also explore the potential implications of these technologies and how they could change the world as we know it.

So, let's get started!

BLOCKCHAIN

CHAPTER 1

HISTORY OF BLOCKCHAIN

Blockchain technology has to be one of the most significant innovations of the 21st century, given the ripple effect it has on various sectors, from finance to manufacturing and education. Unknown to many, the history of Blockchain dates back to the early 1990s.

Since its popularity started growing a few years back, several applications have cropped up, all but underlining the impact it is destined to have as the race for digital economies heats up. In this discussion, we'll learn about the history of Blockchain with Blockchain evolution.

HOW BLOCKCHAIN EMERGE

Stuart Haber and W. Scott Stornetta envisioned what many people have come to know as blockchain in 1991. Their first work involved working on a cryptographically secured chain of blocks whereby no one could tamper with the documents' timestamps.

In 1992, they upgraded their system to incorporate Merkle trees that enhanced efficiency, thereby enabling the collection of more documents on a single block. However, it was in 2008 that Blockchain History started to gain relevance, thanks to the work of one person or group by the name Satoshi Nakamoto.

Satoshi Nakamoto is accredited as the brains behind blockchain technology. Very little is known about Nakamoto as people believe he could be a person or group that worked on Bitcoin, the first application of digital ledger technology.

Nakamoto conceptualized the first blockchain in 2008, from which the technology evolved and found its way into many applications beyond cryptocurrencies. Satoshi Nakamoto released the first whitepaper about the technology in 2009. In the whitepaper, he provided details of how the technology was well equipped to enhance digital trust given the decentralization aspect, which meant nobody would ever be in control of anything.

Since Satoshi Nakamoto exited the scene and handed over Bitcoin development to other core developers, the digital ledger technology has evolved, resulting in new applications that make up the blockchain History.

BLOCKCHAIN STRUCTURE

In simple terms, a Blockchain is a peer-to-peer distributed ledger that is secure and used to record transactions across many computers. The ledger's contents can only be updated by adding another block linked to the previous block. It can also be envisioned as a peer-to-peer network running on top of the internet.

In layman's or business's terms, blockchain is a platform where people are allowed to carry out transactions of all sorts without the need for a central or trusted arbitrator.

The created database is shared among network participants transparently, whereby everyone can access its contents. Database management is done autonomously using peer-to-peer networks and a time stamping server. Each block in a blockchain is arranged to reference the previous block's content.

The blocks that form a blockchain hold batches of transactions approved by participants in a network. Each block comes with a cryptographic hash of a previous block in the chain.

EVOLUTION OF BLOCKCHAIN: PHASE 1- TRANSACTIONS

2008-2013: Blockchain 1.0: Bitcoin Emergence

Most people believe that Bitcoin and Blockchain are the same things. However, that is not the case, as one is the underlying technology that powers most applications, one of which is cryptocurrencies.

Bitcoin came into being in 2008 as the first application of Blockchain technology. Satoshi Nakamoto, in his whitepaper, detailed it as an electronic peer-to-peer system. Nakamoto formed the genesis block, from which other blocks were mined and interconnected, resulting in one of the largest chains of blocks carrying different pieces of information and transactions.

Since Bitcoin, an application of blockchain, hit the airwaves, several applications have cropped up, all seeking to leverage the principles and capabilities of digital ledger technology. Consequently, blockchain history contains a long list of applications that have come into being with the evolution of technology.

EVOLUTION OF BLOCKCHAIN: PHASE 2- CONTRACTS

2013-2015: Blockchain 2.0: Ethereum Development

In a world where innovation is the order of the day, Vitalik Buterin is among a growing list of developers who felt Bitcoin had not yet reached there when it came to leveraging the full capabilities of blockchain technology as one of the first contributors to the Bitcoin codebase.

Concerned by Bitcoin's limitations, Buterin started working on what he felt would be a malleable blockchain that could perform various functions in addition to being a peer-to-peer network. Ethereum was born out as a new public blockchain in 2013 with added functionalities compared to Bitcoin, a development that has turned out to be a pivotal moment in Blockchain history.

Buterin differentiated Ethereum from Bitcoin Blockchain by enabling a function that allows people to record other assets such as slogans and contracts. The new feature expanded Ethereum functionalities from being a cryptocurrency to a platform for developing decentralized applications.

Officially launched in 2015, Ethereum blockchain has evolved to become one of the most significant applications of blockchain technology, given its ability to support smart contracts that perform various functions. Ethereum blockchain platform has also gathered an active developer community that has seen it establish a true ecosystem.

Ethereum blockchain processes the most number of daily transactions thanks to its ability to support smart contracts and decentralized applications. Its market cap has also increased significantly in the cryptocurrency space.

EVOLUTION OF BLOCKCHAIN: PHASE 3- APPLICATIONS

2018: Blockchain 3.0: the Future

Blockchain History and evolution do not stop with Ethereum and Bitcoin. Several projects have cropped up in recent years, leveraging blockchain technology capabilities. New projects have sought to address some of the deficiencies of Bitcoin and Ethereum and develop new features leveraging blockchain capabilities.

Some new blockchain applications include NEO, billed as the first open-source, decentralized, and blockchain platform launched in China. Even though the country has banned cryptocurrencies, it remains active in blockchain innovations. NEO casts itself as the Chinese Ethereum, having already received the backing of Alibaba CEO Jack Ma as it plots to have the same impact as Baidu in the country.

In the race to accelerate the development of the Internet of Things, some developers, so it fit, leveraged blockchain technology and, in the process, came up with IOTA. The cryptocurrency platform is optimized for the Internet of things ecosystem as it strives to provide zero transaction fees and unique verification processes. It also addresses some of the scalability issues associated with Blockchain 1.0 Bitcoin.

In addition to IOTA and NEO, other second-generation blockchain platforms also have a ripple effect in the sector. Monero Zcash and Dash blockchains came into being to address some of the security and scalability issues associated with the early blockchain applications. Dubbed as privacy Altcoins, the three blockchain platforms seek to provide high levels of privacy and security regarding transactions.

The blockchain history discussed above involves public blockchain networks, whereby anyone can access the contents of a network. However, with the evolution of technology, several companies have started adopting technology internally to enhance operational efficiency.

Large enterprises are investing big in hiring professionals as they seek to gain a head start on the use of technology. Companies like Microsoft and Microsoft appear to have taken the lead in exploring blockchain technology applications, resulting in what has become known as private, hybrid, and federated blockchains.

CHAPTER 2

INTRODUCTION TO BLOCKCHAIN

Blockchain is the innovative database technology at the heart of nearly all cryptocurrencies. By distributing identical copies of a database across an entire network, blockchain makes it very difficult to hack or cheat the system. While cryptocurrency is the most popular use for blockchain presently, the technology offers the potential to serve an extensive range of applications.

Blockchain is a distributed digital ledger that stores data of any kind. A blockchain can record information about cryptocurrency transactions, NFT ownership, or Defi smart contracts.

While any conventional database can store this information, blockchain is unique because it's decentralized. Rather than being maintained in one location by a centralized administrator, think of an Excel spreadsheet or a bank database—many identical copies of a blockchain database are held on multiple computers across a network. These individual computers are referred to as nodes.

HOW DOES BLOCKCHAIN WORK?

The blockchain is hardly accidental: The digital ledger is often described as a "chain" of individual "blocks" of data. As fresh data is periodically added to the network, a new "block" is created and attached to the "chain." This involves all nodes updating their version of the blockchain ledger to be identical.

How these new blocks are created is key to why blockchain is considered highly secure. Most nodes must verify and confirm the legitimacy of the new data before a new block can be added to the ledger. For a cryptocurrency, they might ensure that new transactions in a block were not fraudulent or that coins had not been spent more than once. This differs from a standalone database or spreadsheet, where one person can make changes without oversight.

"Once there is consensus, the block is added to the chain, and the underlying transactions are recorded in the distributed ledger.

Transactions are typically secured using cryptography, meaning the nodes must solve complex mathematical equations to process a transaction.

PUBLIC BLOCKCHAINS VS. PRIVATE BLOCKCHAINS

There are both public and private blockchains. In a public blockchain, anyone can participate, meaning they can read, write or audit the data on the blockchain. Notably, altering transactions logged in a public blockchain is difficult as no single authority controls the nodes.

A private blockchain, meanwhile, is controlled by an organization or group. Only it can decide who is invited to the system; it has the authority to go back and alter the blockchain. This private blockchain process is more similar to an in-house data storage system except spread over multiple nodes to increase security.

HOW BLOCKCHAIN IS USED

Blockchain technology is used for many purposes, from financial services to voting systems.

CRYPTOCURRENCY

The most common use of blockchain today is as the backbone of cryptocurrencies, like Bitcoin or Ethereum. The transactions are recorded on a blockchain when people buy, exchange, or spend cryptocurrency. The more people use cryptocurrency; the more widespread blockchain could become.

Cryptocurrencies are volatile; they are not yet used much to purchase goods and services. But that is changing as PayPal, Square, and other money service businesses make digital asset services broadly available to vendors and retail customers.

BANKING

Beyond cryptocurrency, blockchain processes transactions in fiat currency, like dollars and euros. This could be faster than sending money through a bank or other financial institution, as the transactions can be verified more quickly and processed outside normal business hours.

ASSET TRANSFERS

Blockchain can also be used to record and transfer the ownership of different assets. This is currently very popular with digital assets like NFTs, representing ownership of digital art and videos.

However, blockchain could also be used to process the ownership of real-life assets, like the deed to real estate and vehicles. The two sides of a party would first use the blockchain to verify that one owns the property and the other has the money to buy; then, they could complete and record the sale on the blockchain.

Using this process, they could transfer the property deed without manually submitting paperwork to update the local county's government records; it would be instantaneously updated in the blockchain.

SMART CONTRACTS

Another blockchain innovation is self-executing contracts, commonly called "smart contracts." These digital contracts are enacted automatically once conditions are met. For instance, a payment for a good might be released instantly once the buyer and seller have met all specified parameters for a deal.

We see great potential in smart contracts—using blockchain technology and coded instructions to automate legal contracts. A properly coded smart legal contract on a distributed ledger can minimize or eliminate the need for outside third parties to verify performance.

SUPPLY CHAIN MONITORING

Supply chains involve massive amounts of information, especially as goods go from one part of the world. With traditional data storage methods, it can be hard to trace the source of problems, like which vendor's poor-quality goods came from. Storing this information on the blockchain would make it easier to go back and monitor the supply chain, such as with IBM's Food Trust, which uses blockchain technology to track food from its harvest to its consumption.

VOTING

Experts are looking into ways to apply blockchain to prevent fraud in voting. In theory, blockchain voting would allow people to submit votes that couldn't be tampered with, as well as would remove the need to have people manually collect and verify paper ballots.

CHAPTER 3

THE PROS AND CONS OF BLOCKCHAIN

Blockchain technology can be seen as taking it to another level by enabling people who would typically not have any affiliation with each other to collaborate and transact value. This Chapter will discuss the major pros and cons of Blockchain technology in depth.

ADVANTAGES OF BLOCKCHAIN.

There are many advantages of blockchain technology. Below are some key benefits:

HIGHER ACCURACY OF TRANSACTIONS

Because multiple nodes must verify a blockchain transaction, this can reduce error. If one node has a mistake in the database, the others would see it's different and catch the error.

In contrast, in a traditional database, if someone makes a mistake, it may be more likely to go through. In addition, every asset is individually identified and tracked on the blockchain ledger, so there is no chance of double spending it (like a person overdrawing their bank account, thereby spending money twice).

NO SINGLE POINT OF FAILURE

Blockchain technology distributes data throughout a network of computers rather than storing it in one central location. This makes the system much more resistant to hacking or corruption because there is no "single point of failure" that hackers can exploit.

NO NEED FOR INTERMEDIARIES

Using blockchain, two parties in a transaction can confirm and complete something without working through a third party. This saves time and the cost of paying for an intermediary like a bank.

It can bring greater efficiency to all digital commerce, increase financial empowerment to the unbanked or underbanked populations of the world, and power a new generation of internet applications as a result.

EXTRA SECURITY

Theoretically, a decentralized network, like a blockchain, makes it nearly impossible for someone to make fraudulent transactions. To enter forged transactions, they must hack every node and change every ledger. While this isn't necessarily impossible, many cryptocurrency blockchain systems use proof-of-stake or proof-of-work transaction verification methods, making it difficult and not in participants' best interests to add fraudulent transactions.

MORE EFFICIENT TRANSFERS

Since blockchains operate 24/7, people can make more efficient financial and asset transfers, especially internationally. They don't need to wait days for a bank or a government agency to confirm everything manually.

CONS OF BLOCKCHAIN TECHNOLOGY

There are also a few disadvantages of blockchain technology that are worth mentioning. Here are a few of them:

LIMIT ON TRANSACTIONS PER SECOND

Since blockchain depends on a more extensive network to approve transactions, there's a limit to how quickly it can move. For example, with Visa, Bitcoin can only process 4.6 transactions per second versus 1,700 per second. In addition, increasing numbers of transactions can create network speed issues. Until this improves, scalability is a challenge.

HIGH ENERGY COSTS

Having all the nodes working to verify transactions takes significantly more electricity than a single database or spreadsheet. Not only does this make blockchain-based transactions more expensive, but it also creates a significant carbon burden on the environment.

Because of this, some industry leaders are beginning to move away from certain blockchain technologies, like Bitcoin: For instance, Elon Musk recently said Tesla would stop accepting Bitcoin partly because he was concerned about the environmental damage.

RISK OF ASSET LOSS

Some digital assets are secured using a cryptographic key, like cryptocurrency in a blockchain wallet. You need to guard this key carefully.

"If the owner of a digital asset loses the private cryptographic key that gives them access to their asset, currently there is no way to recover it—the asset is gone permanently," says Gray. Because the system is decentralized, you can't call a central authority, like your bank, to ask to regain access.

POTENTIAL FOR ILLEGAL ACTIVITY

Blockchain's decentralization adds more privacy and confidentiality, which, unfortunately, makes it appealing to criminals. It's harder to track illicit transactions on the blockchain through bank transactions tied to a name.

LACK OF REGULATION

The cryptocurrency and blockchain industries are still largely unregulated. This means there's more potential for fraudsters to take advantage of investors. The U.S. Securities and Exchange Commission (SEC) is starting to bring some clarity by classifying some digital assets as securities that fall under existing securities regulations. But this is just the beginning—the SEC has said it will continue to monitor the space closely.

Before investing in any crypto asset or project, you should be aware of these disadvantages of blockchain technology. As with any new technology, there are risks and challenges associated with its adoption and implementation. But despite these challenges, many believe that blockchain has the potential to revolutionize the way we do business and interact with the world.

CHAPTER 4

THE FUTURE OF BLOCKCHAIN

The future of blockchain is shrouded in potential but fraught with uncertainty. But despite the many challenges facing the technology, there's reason to believe that blockchain will become increasingly important in the years to come.

Blockchain technologies could significantly influence the financial industry in the future. Traceable global money with an efficient infrastructure would not just result in significant cost savings for all market participants, but it will also change international banking. Bitcoin will revolutionize payments as email changes communication and the underlying blockchain technology could significantly impact other industries, such as supply chain management, voting, and identity verification.

We will likely see more widespread adoption of blockchain technologies in the coming years. And as technology matures, it will become increasingly important in our lives. So it's essential to stay informed about the latest developments in blockchain and cryptocurrency.

WHAT IS CHANGING?

As you are aware, blockchain is already gaining popularity. But it's also starting to question procedures in commercial fields. In reality, several industries are discovering that blockchain technology is superior to the methods used for fulfilling crucial tasks. Let's examine the five key industries that blockchain technology is influencing.

BANKING

Assume you use a traditional bank to transfer your friend $100. You're only sending her $90 because the bank charges you a $10 fee. She will receive considerably less if she is abroad due to hidden fees and transfer rates. Overall, the procedure is costly and time-consuming; it also cannot be completely guaranteed to be secure.

On the other hand, the commercial banking system is challenged by blockchain since it offers a peer-to-peer payment method with high security and minimal fees. You are not required to pay a central authority since there is none. What a cool thing! By doing this, a transaction using a cryptocurrency, such as Bitcoin or one of the many others, can be made without the involvement of a third party. Giving you real sovereignty over your transaction, your payment to your friend is recorded in a ledger that any bitcoin user may access.

CYBERSECURITY

The biggest threat to our digital world is cyberattacks. When Equifax revealed its massive data breach in 2017 that affected 143 billion consumers, look what happened to our data: we went nuts. Such nightmares can be put to a stop by blockchain technology. It can protect our data from alteration and illegal access.

Blockchain is the best technology for areas requiring excellent security because it is a decentralized system. As a result, there is NO SINGLE POINT OF ENTRY for a large-scale assault because all the data held on a bitcoin or other blockchain network is authenticated and encrypted using a cryptographic algorithm. Blockchain also makes it simple to detect harmful data attacks because of peer-to-peer links, which prevent data from being changed or tampered with. Blockchain also offers a safe and transparent means to record transactions without revealing private information to anyone by doing away with a central authority. Guardtime is one business that successfully employs cybersecurity in this manner. We anticipate numerous businesses will copy it in light of its success and further disrupt this sector.

SUPPLY CHAIN MANAGEMENT

If you ordered food, delivered it, and later discovered it repulsive, you could use blockchain technology to track every stage of the supply chain. The owner of the business from which you made the transaction might review his blockchain ledger in the past and determine where exactly in the supply chain the order went wrong, displeasing you. He might start with the farmer and work his way up to the producer, distributor, retailer, and finally, you, the consumer. In other words, blockchain in supply chain management offers ongoing validation and transparency of shared transactions amongst numerous supply chain stakeholders. Because all transactions are irreversible and verifiable, it is simple for an owner or client to inspect each record.

HEALTHCARE

The preservation of people's health information today is fraught with numerous issues. Because everything is stored in centralized files, anyone can access this extremely private data. It can take hours to find the correct file when someone asks someone else for their information; this creates the potential for data breaches, theft, or other losses. Blockchain technology is crucial in this sector for this reason.

Here, blockchain technology does away with the requirement for centralized authority and allows quick data access. In this case, it is challenging for a hacker to alter the data because each block is interconnected with every other block and dispersed among the blockchain nodes. Information from personal medical files must be kept confidential at all costs.

Blockchain technology can also manage medication fraud is a further issue in healthcare. The issue is that it can frequently be challenging to distinguish between genuine and counterfeit drugs. This issue is resolved by blockchain technology's use of supply chain management protocols, which allow for the provenance of medicines to be tracked.

Using blockchain technology, United Healthcare has increased medical records' privacy, security, and interoperability. As a result, it has noticed a significant improvement in its operations. We anticipate that as more healthcare organizations decentralize their operations, more will do the same.

GOVERNMENT

Voter fraud can be eliminated by blockchain technology. Most voters cast ballots in person or by mail in a typical election. A local authority must then count the votes. Online voting is feasible in this scenario as well, but just like in the other businesses we've mentioned, difficulties with fraud occur since a central authority is used.

Thus, utilizing blockchain technology becomes the best option. Here, voters can conveniently cast ballots online without disclosing their identity. Because each ID can only be connected to one vote, blockchain technology allows for the most precise counting of ballots. With blockchain technology, fraud is virtually impossible. Thus it cannot happen. Additionally, a vote recorded in a ledger cannot be altered or removed.

INSURANCE

The decentralized blockchain technology system allows insurers to identify false claims and prevent forgeries easily. In the past, individuals have taken out insurance policies and filed false claims. With blockchain technology, each transaction is verified and recorded. This makes it difficult for an individual to commit fraud because all the information is there for anyone to see.

Additionally, smart contracts can be used in insurance. A smart contract is a contract that is written in code and stored on the blockchain. It automatically executes when certain conditions are met. For example, if you took out an insurance policy that covered your car in the event of an accident, the smart contract would automatically pay out the money to you if your car was damaged. This would eliminate the need for you to file a claim and wait for it to be processed.

TRANSPORTATION

The transportation industry can use blockchain technology to trace the shipment of goods and prevent fraud. In the past, it has been difficult to track the shipment of goods because no central system recorded all the information. With blockchain technology, each transaction is recorded on a public ledger. This allows anyone to see where the goods are at any given time.

Additionally, blockchain technology can be used to create a digital ID for each driver. This would allow for the tracking of driver behavior and improve safety. For example, if a driver had a history of accidents, that information would be available to other drivers, and they could choose to avoid it.

Digital IDs would also allow for the tracking of mileage driven. This would benefit insurance companies because they could offer lower rates to drivers who drove less. It would also benefit the environment by incentivizing people to drive less.

CRYPTOCURRENCIES

CHAPTER 5

HISTORY OF CRYPTOCURRENCIES

First and foremost, cryptocurrencies are digital currencies decentralized and not controlled by any government. The history of cryptocurrencies dates back 1980s, when cryptocurrencies were called cyber currencies.

Interestingly, these coins started gaining in popularity more than a decade ago, in 2008, with the introduction of Bitcoin. The cryptocurrency mentioned earlier was created by an anonymous programmer or group of programmers under Satoshi Nakamoto.

Since the cryptocurrency launch mentioned above in 2009, cryptocurrencies have been all the rage. Over the last several years, their popularity has only grown, with more and more people investing in them.

The cryptocurrency was first mentioned in the 1980s, more precisely in 1989. However, it was only in the early 1990s that cryptographic protocols, as well as software, began to be developed that would enable the creation of a truly decentralized digital currency.

In 2008, Satoshi Nakamoto (a pseudonym) published a paper. It outlined a system for creating a digital currency that didn't require trust in any third party. Satoshi Nakamoto's paper practically launched the cryptocurrency revolution.

WHAT ARE CRYPTOCURRENCIES, AND HOW DO THEY WORK?

Cryptocurrency is a digital payment system that doesn't rely on banks to verify transactions. A peer-to-peer system enables anyone to send and receive payments anywhere. Instead of being physical money carried around and exchanged in the real world, cryptocurrency payments exist purely as digital entries to an online database describing specific transactions. The transactions are recorded in a public ledger when you transfer cryptocurrency funds. Cryptocurrency is stored in digital wallets.

Cryptocurrency received its name because it uses encryption to verify transactions. This means advanced coding is involved in storing and transmitting cryptocurrency data between wallets and public ledgers. Encryption aims to provide security and safety.

The first cryptocurrency was Bitcoin, founded in 2009, and is the best known today. Much of the interest in cryptocurrencies is to trade for profit, with speculators at times driving prices skyward.

A cryptocurrency is a form of digital currency in which encryption techniques regulate the generation of units and verify the transfer of funds, operating independently from central banks. There has been much speculation as to whether Cryptocurrency will one day completely replace physical fiat money (paper bills) or even just paper checks. While it's improbable that this would happen, people worldwide still have widespread interest who want an alternative way to pay for goods and services without confidence in their local currencies.

Cryptocurrencies like Bitcoin have no physical backing whatsoever: only users trust that other users won't betray them by abusing these features [of anonymity]. So if you use Bitcoin, don't spend more than you're willing to lose because there's no telling whether Cryptocurrencies will still be around tomorrow.

Cryptocurrency is a new kind of money that works entirely differently from conventional currency. The most fundamental difference between them is that they are purely virtual currencies, which means there are no physical cryptocurrency coins or bills you may keep in your pocket.

It's also generated in a unique method. Instead of being produced by a central bank or government, as are fiat currencies such as the U.S. dollar and euro, new cryptocurrency units usually enter circulation through a technical process that involves the participation of volunteers from all over the world using their computers.

HOW CRYPTOCURRENCY WORK

While cryptocurrencies are used to exchange or store value, they all rely on Blockchain - a specific kind of public ledger technology - to keep track of data and record all transactions that flow through the network.

A blockchain is a digital blockchain containing batches of transactions and other data, like what it sounds like. Once each block has been added to the chain, it becomes irreversible, ensuring that any data stored within it cannot be altered or removed. A blockchain network's integrity can only be maintained if everyone participating honestly records new data and adds it to the Ledger.

The nodes perform a variety of roles on the network, from storing a complete archive of all historical transactions to validating new transaction data. By having a distributed group of people all maintaining their copy of the ledger, blockchain technology has the following advantages over traditional finance, where a single institution supports a master copy:

- There is no single point of failure: If one node fails, it has zero impact on the blockchain ledger.
- There is no single source of truth that can be easily corrupted.
- The nodes collectively manage the database and confirm that new entries are valid transactions.

Consider it like having a group of computers take the place of a bank, continually updating users' balance sheets. In contrast, distributed ledgers maintain the balance sheets on numerous servers rather than in a single location. The balance sheets are divided into many copies and stored on multiple computers across several nodes, each acting as a separate server. As a result, even if one of the computers goes down, it won't be as bad as losing access to a server-based database that can happen in traditional financial systems.

Cryptocurrencies can avoid the security flaws that plague fiat currencies because of this infrastructural design. It's difficult to attack or tamper with this system since the attackers must gain control of at least 50% of the computers connected to the blockchain network. Depending on the extensive network, carrying out a concerted assault might be prohibitively expensive. If you compare the amount required to attack established cryptocurrencies like bitcoin to what the attacker stands to gain at the end of the day, pursuing such an endeavor wouldn't be feasible financially.

Also, it should be noted that their decentralized nature contributes to the censorship resistance of these cryptocurrencies. Cryptocurrencies are distinct from banks in that their databases are distributed worldwide rather than regulated by a government. As a result, when a government shuts down one of these computers or all of the computers within its authority, the network continues to operate because there may be thousands of additional nodes outside its reach.

HOW TO FIND COINS TO INVEST IN

The first thing you need to know is how to find coins with great potential for a significant increase in value. This can be done in several ways, but the easiest way would be to research social media sites such as Twitter or Reddit. You will see many people who claim certain coins will go up dramatically. Then those same people share links with the coin's wallet address so others can send them money. These tweets usually have hashtags like #HODL which means Hold On for Dear Life, because they believe their prediction was correct. They hope it goes higher than what they paid within a short time frame, so they want new investors to buy into it at this low price point before everyone starts buying, making the price go up.

- CoinMarketCap is an excellent place to start. The website lists the top 100 coins by market capitalization, price, and volume. - It provides a quick overview of what's available without too much detail on any coin or platform. You'll need more than that if you want to buy anything! For that reason, we recommend checking out our list of exchanges for beginners below so you can find which one best suits your needs...

- Some resources will provide information about cryptocurrency investment strategies. Still, they are all reasonably similar: acquire as many coins as possible at low prices before their value increases due to increased demand/limited supply (and consequent price rise). This strategy requires researching the past and future performance of the coins you are considering. You can also diversify your portfolio by picking platforms with different features and trading pairs, which is beyond this guide's scope.

CHAPTER 6

MAIN TYPES OF CRYPTOCURRENCIES

The term "altcoin" refers to other individual cryptocurrencies other than Bitcoin, which is regarded as the first cryptocurrency ever developed (a combo word derived from "alternative coin"). It's hard to determine which cryptocurrencies are the best, but because of their scalability, anonymity, and the range of functionality they support, Bitcoin and some of the most prominent altcoins available are top choices.

Since each cryptocurrency has unique features, depending on what the developer intended it for, there isn't one "greatest" cryptocurrency. Below is an overview of some of the most widely used digital coins.

1. BITCOIN

As the first decentralized cryptocurrency to use blockchain technology to enable payments and online transactions, Bitcoin is known. The blockchain of Bitcoin serves as a public ledger of all transactions in the history of Bitcoin, replacing the need for a central bank to regulate the money supply in an economy (like the Federal Reserve working with the U.S. Department of the Treasury) or independent parties to confirm transactions.

The ledger enables a party to demonstrate ownership of the Bitcoin they are attempting to use and may help stop fraud and other unauthorized manipulation of the money. Peer-to-peer money transfers (such as those between participants in two different countries) can also be quicker and less expensive with a decentralized currency than with a standard currency exchange that involves a third-party entity

2. ETHER (ETHEREUM)

The Ethereum network's official coin for transactions is called ether. Smart contracts and other decentralized applications can be created on the Ethereum platform using blockchain technology, which eliminates the need for software to be distributed on app exchanges like Apple's (NASDAQ: AAPL) App Store or Alphabet's (NASDAQ: GOOGL)(NASDAQ: GOOG) Google Play Store, where the tech giants may receive a 30% cut of any sales. Ethereum is a software development sandbox and a cryptocurrency (the actual currencies are measured in units called Ether).

3. TETER

The cryptocurrency Tether is a stablecoin or pegged to a fiat currency, in this case, the dollar. The concept behind Tether is to combine the advantages of a cryptocurrency with the stability of a currency issued by a sovereign government, such as the lack of the need for financial intermediaries (versus the wild price fluctuations inherent with many cryptos).

4. BINANCE COIN

On the Binance cryptocurrency exchange platform, Binance Coin is accessible along with other trading digital coins. Although it can be used as a form of payment, Binance Coin also enables tokens that can be used to cover exchange costs and power Binance's DEX (decentralized exchange) for the development of apps.

5. USD COIN

Another stablecoin is USD Coin, which is tied to the dollar, just like Tether. USD Coin is housed on the Ethereum blockchain, just like Tether. The goal of the USD Coin was to develop a "totally digital" dollar with the same level of stability as U.S. fiat money but without the need for a bank account or residence in a particular nation. USD Coin is intended to be used as regular money to make purchases from online retailers rather than as an investment.

CHAPTER 7

BUYING CRYPTOCURRENCY

You may be wondering how to buy cryptocurrency safely. There are typically three steps involved. These are:

STEP 1: CHOOSING A PLATFORM

The first step is deciding which platform to use. Generally, you can choose between a traditional broker or a dedicated cryptocurrency exchange:

Traditional brokers: These are online brokers who offer ways to buy and sell cryptocurrency and other financial assets like stocks, bonds, and ETFs. These platforms tend to offer lower trading costs but fewer crypto features.

Cryptocurrency exchanges: There are many cryptocurrency exchanges, each offering different cryptocurrencies, wallet storage, interest-bearing account options, and more. Many exchanges charge asset-based fees.

When comparing different platforms, consider which cryptocurrencies are on offer, what fees they charge, their security features, storage and withdrawal options, and any educational resources.

STEP 2: FUNDING YOUR ACCOUNT

Once you have chosen your platform, the next step is to fund your account so you can begin trading. Most crypto exchanges allow users to purchase crypto using fiat (i.e., government-issued) currencies such as the US Dollar, the British Pound, or the Euro using their debit or credit cards – although this varies by platform.

Crypto purchases with credit cards are considered risky, and some exchanges don't support them. Some credit card companies don't allow crypto transactions either. This is because cryptocurrencies are highly volatile, and it is not advisable to risk going into debt — or potentially paying high credit card transaction fees — for certain assets.

Some platforms will also accept ACH transfers and wire transfers. The accepted payment methods and time taken for deposits or withdrawals differ per platform. Equally, the time taken for deposits to clear varies by payment method.

An essential factor to consider is fees. These include potential deposit and withdrawal transaction fees plus trading fees. Fees will vary by payment method and platform, which is something to research at the outset.

STEP 3: PLACING AN ORDER

You can place an order via your broker's or exchange's web or mobile platform. If you plan to buy cryptocurrencies, you can select "buy," choose the order type, enter the number of cryptocurrencies you want to purchase and confirm the order. The exact process applies to "sell" orders.

There are also other ways to invest in crypto. These include payment services like PayPal, Cash App, and Venmo, which allow users to buy, sell, or hold cryptocurrencies. In addition, there are the following investment vehicles:

Bitcoin trusts: You can buy shares of Bitcoin trusts with a regular brokerage account. These vehicles give retail investors exposure to crypto through the stock market.

Bitcoin mutual funds: There are Bitcoin ETFs and mutual funds to choose from.

Blockchain stocks or ETFs: You can also indirectly invest in crypto through blockchain companies specializing in the technology behind crypto and crypto transactions. Alternatively, you can buy stocks or ETFs from blockchain technology companies.

CHAPTER 8

BUYING WITH CRYPTOCURRENCY

When it was first launched, Bitcoin was intended to be a medium for daily transactions, making it possible to buy everything from a cup of coffee to a computer or even big-ticket items like real estate. That hasn't quite materialized, and while the number of institutions accepting cryptocurrencies is growing, large transactions involving them are rare.

Using a cryptocurrency debit card is the simplest way to make purchases using bitcoin. These cards already have your preferred cryptocurrency loaded on them. You spend cryptocurrency, and the store gets paid in fiat. To ensure these transactions go smoothly, cryptocurrency debit cards collaborate with industry leaders in payment processing like Mastercard and Visa.

Even while the number of organizations accepting bitcoin is expanding daily, significant transactions involving it are still uncommon. For instance, there aren't many records of cryptocurrencies used in real estate transactions. Nevertheless, it is possible to use bitcoin to make various purchases through e-commerce websites. Some of the most popular categories are shown below.

CAR DEALERSHIPS

Bitcoin is already accepted as payment at several vehicle dealerships. The list includes luxury car sellers that sell Lamborghinis (a favorite among bitcoiners) and more practical car dealers that sell Subarus. Tesla has emerged as the most critical and recent name to join the group of businesses that allow you to buy cars using cryptocurrencies. Elon Musk, the founder of Tesla, favors bitcoin and is a crypto phile.

Musk announced Tesla would accept bitcoin as payment in a tweet from March 2021.

A few months later, Musk tweeted that Tesla was discontinuing bitcoin payments due to environmental concerns.

TECHNOLOGY AND E-COMMERCE PRODUCT

On their websites, several businesses that primarily sell tech products accept bitcoin. Newegg, AT&T, and Microsoft are a few of them.

Only the Microsoft online store presently supports bitcoin; the Xbox gaming platform is not one of them. Additionally, it forbids placing adverts on its website that promote cryptocurrencies or products related to them.

Starting in 2014, Overstock, an e-commerce site with a broad selection of products, was one of the first to accept bitcoin; its creator, Patrick Byrne, was a pioneer in the field.

Using bitcoin, you can buy goods from many other websites, both large and small. Shopify and the well-known Japanese e-commerce company Rakuten are two examples.

The largest online store in the world, Amazon, and eBay, are notable holdouts today. Amazon had no plans to work with bitcoin as early as 2014.

This resistance is perplexing given that the company-owned platforms, such as Twitch, permit and even promote the use of bitcoin.

Following the surge in bitcoin values in 2017, eBay considered enabling cryptocurrency use on its site. It has even invested in big banner ads for bitcoin conferences. However, the San Jose,

California-based business declined to say whether it would sanction cryptocurrency-based transactions in 2019.

JEWELRY AND EXPENSIVE WATCHES

Many manufacturers and sellers of luxury products have started accepting bitcoin payments. In exchange for bitcoin and other cryptocurrencies, Rolex, Patek Philippe, and other premium timepieces are available from the online luxury merchant BitDials.

A watch made by upscale watchmaker Franck Muller even featured a QR code taken from the bitcoin genesis block and was covered in gold and diamonds.

Some jewelry retailers have joined with payment processors to enable cryptocurrency-based transactions from their stores.

NEWS MEDIA

Most crypto-media outlets accept bitcoin as payment for subscriptions or other services. The Chicago Sun-Times was one of the first well-known publications to accept bitcoin on its platform in 2014.

Publisher of periodicals Time Inc. started taking cryptocurrency payments for digital subscriptions in the same year. The magazine publisher and Crypto.com established new cryptocurrency cooperation in 2019.

INSURANCE

The insurance sector has, for the most part, adopted cryptocurrency slowly. However, things are starting to alter. Although life insurance remains off-limits, insurance companies have started taking bitcoin payments for premiums on other products in their portfolio.

For instance, Swiss insurer AXA stated in April 2021 that it has started taking bitcoin as a form of payment for all of its insurance lines except for life insurance (due to regulatory issues).

The "pay-per-mile" auto insurance broker Metromile also takes bitcoin for premium payments.

CHAPTER 9

DIVERSIFYING YOUR PORTFOLIO

As you already know, diversification is paramount to success in almost every facet of life. It may be interesting to look into if you have only one investment, but if that investment crashes, so will your funds. Cryptocurrencies are no different. Suppose you invest all of your money into just one cryptocurrency. In that case, there is a chance that the price will go up or down, which either makes you very happy or extremely sad. Diversifying decreases this risk by spreading around your investments, so there are fewer chances for any single event to harm your portfolio. There are several ways to diversify, but let's explore how it can be done with cryptocurrencies as an example. The first step would be deciding whether or not to use multiple exchanges and how many. The next step would be deciding on a portfolio and how to split it up.

The primary risks of not having a diverse portfolio.

There are several reasons to diversify one's cryptocurrency portfolio. The following is a list of the most important ones:

1. Diversifying your portfolio reduces the risks of a collapse in any particular cryptocurrency by spreading it out over multiple cryptocurrencies and industries.
2. Diversifying your portfolio is also a great way to increase your exposure to various cryptocurrencies. If one of the cryptocurrencies in your portfolio grows substantially, you will be thankful for having it there.

3. Another reason to diversify is that if all of your eggs are in one basket and something happens, so is everything you own or have worked towards up until that point.

4. Market forces and community sentiment drive cryptocurrencies such as Bitcoin and Ether. As a result, even if you believe a particular cryptocurrency has strong value propositions and isn't overvalued, its price is unlikely to follow suit or endure for an extended time. This implies that having many financial investments will help protect your money from losses when everyone starts selling due to fear, panic, or FOMO.

5. Cryptocurrency markets are global, and many cryptocurrencies are subject to specific nations or industries. Ripple (XRP) is linked to the banking sector, for example. Before investing in a coin, you should always check whether its community and underlying project focus on some geographical regions or special interest groups.

6. What might persuade you into thinking that every cryptocurrency will continue to rise indefinitely when there is a bull trend in the cryptocurrency market? This isn't accurate; not all cryptos may maintain their present prices if they become common money currencies due to market forces alone. As a result, having numerous portfolios helps you avoid these dangers.

7. According to seasoned traders, diversification within your trading portfolio increases the likelihood of greater profits. The same is true for bitcoin portfolios; you won't be able to get the most out of your

investments if they're all invested in the same cryptocurrency.

8. Because most cryptocurrencies are linked to the value of Bitcoin, having a short position in BTC helps ensure your investment isn't harmed by volatility in cryptocurrency markets. Even if all other currencies fall in value, you won't lose out since BTC will help absorb some of these losses.
9. Investors and traders may profit from diversification effects by trading individual cryptos against each other or into fiat currency when they have more alternatives.

USING MULTIPLE EXCHANGES WHEN DIVERSIFYING

It's essential to use several exchanges when diversifying because you don't rely too much on any particular exchange crashing or having problems with withdrawals/deposits. Which exchanges should you use? It's up to you, but I would recommend more than three different ones, at least more if possible. Even using five other exchanges is better than using just one. The more exchanges you use, the higher your chances are of finding a reasonable price for any particular cryptocurrency at some point in time.

The following are several examples of different portfolio splits that can be used when diversifying.

EQUAL/EASY TO CALCULATE –

Using an equal split is very easy since you don't have to think about percentages, just how much money you want to invest into each cryptocurrency. This makes it easier to figure out how much money goes where but this also means that if one coin doubles in value and the other doesn't grow at all, then the former will have twice as much money invested as the latter, so there's less a chance for them both to succeed.

FAIR –

A fair split means you distribute your investments based on some system you have come up with, for example, a 70-20-10 percent split. In the case of this percentage distribution, it would mean investing 70% of your money into one particular cryptocurrency, 20% into another, and 10% into a third one. The more complex the percentages are, the harder they will be to keep track of in your head or on paper. Still, if done correctly, this can result in excellent diversification. Why is this considered "fair" instead of equal? Each coin would get 33% in an equal division, while one gets 70% here. It's not exactly fair, but since this isn't meant to make anyone rich overnight, it's more than enough.

COMPLEX –

The most complex one would be to split the portfolio according to some percentage you've come up with. For example, suppose you distribute your investments based on a 60-30-10% split. In that case, one of the cryptocurrencies gets 60%, another gets 30%, and the last gets 10%. It's hard to choose what those percentages should be. Still, they must be all different. Otherwise, this wouldn't be diversification anymore and instead just equal division. Even though the percentages might not be equal, their total is.

A final thing to consider when diversifying is whether or not to invest in ICOs (Initial Coin Offerings) and industries such as finance, healthcare, and technology. What's the point of investing in cryptocurrencies if you don't have any money left? Diversification doesn't only mean spreading your investments among different cryptocurrencies; it should also include other industries.

CHAPTER 10

CRYPTOCURRENCY FRAUD AND SCAMS

Scammers still utilize some tried-and-true scam techniques, but now they want to be paid in cryptocurrencies. One of the most common methods con artists get you to buy bitcoin and deliver it to them is through investment scams. However, scammers also use other strategies, such as posing as companies, authorities, or a romantic interest.

INVESTMENT SCAMS

Investment scams frequently begin on social media or online dating apps or sites and promise that you can "earn tons of money" with "zero risk." Of course, these frauds might also begin with a random text, email, or phone. Additionally, cryptocurrency is crucial in investment scams because it can be used for investments and payments.

Here are some typical investment frauds and tips on how to identify them.

Unexpectedly, a so-called "investment manager" calls you. They promise to grow your money if you buy cryptocurrencies and deposit them into their online account. They direct you to an investment website that appears legitimate, but its claims are false, just like theirs. If you log in, you won't be able to withdraw money from your "investment account" without paying exorbitant fees.

A con artist poses as a famous person who can multiply any cryptocurrency you transfer them. However, celebs aren't getting in touch with you on social media. It's a con artist. Additionally, your money will be lost if you click on an unexpected link they offer or send cryptocurrency to a QR code belonging to a purported celebrity.

An online "love interest" requests money or cryptocurrencies from you to assist with investments. That is a con. Know this: that person is a scammer when they ask you for money or gives investment advice after meeting you on a dating website or app. The suggestions and offers to assist you in investing in cryptocurrencies are all frauds. If you send them cryptocurrency or any other money, it will likely be lost and not returned.

Scammers make money-making promises or large rewards with assured returns. No one can provide those assurances. Much less quickly — much less. Additionally, investing in cryptocurrencies is not "low risk." Therefore, it's a scam if a business or individual says you'll make money. even if there is a celebrity endorsement or positive investor reviews. Those are simple to fake.

Scammers make free-money promises. Free money promises are always false, even though they mention free cash or cryptocurrency.

Con artists make significant assertions without backing or justifications. Regardless of the investment, learn how it operates and inquire where your money is going. That information is something sincere investment managers or advisors wish to share and will support with specifics.

Search online for the company or person's name, the cryptocurrency's name, and words like "review," "scam," or "complaint" before making a cryptocurrency investment. View the comments made by others. Moreover, learn more about other typical investing frauds.

BUSINESS, GOVERNMENT, AND JOB IMPERSONATORS

In a corporate, government, or job impersonation scam, the con artist is a reliable source to persuade you to send them money via cryptocurrency purchases and transfers.

Scammers pose as well-known businesses. When sending these in waves, scammers may claim they are from Amazon, Microsoft, FedEx, your bank, or several other companies. They might contact you through phone, text, email, social media, or even by popping up a warning on your computer. They can claim that there is fraud on your account or that your money is in danger and that the only way to remedy it is to buy a cryptocurrency and send it to them. However, that's a con. You will be linked to a con artist if you click the link in any message, respond to the call, or dial the number displayed in the pop-up.

Scammers pose as new or existing companies to sell fake cryptocurrency coins or tokens. They'll claim that the business is entering cryptocurrency by creating its coin or token. They might produce news stories, social media advertisements, or a sleek website to support everything and dupe people into making purchases. However, cryptocurrency coins and tokens are a fraud that steals money from the buyers. Check online to see if a business has released a coin or token. If it is accurate, it will be widely covered by reputable media.

Scammers pretend to be representatives of the government, the police, or utility providers. They can claim that you have a legal issue, that you owe money, or that your accounts or perks have been suspended during an ongoing inquiry. They advise buying cryptocurrency to solve the problem or safeguard your finances. For "safekeeping," they can instruct you to transmit the item to a wallet address they provide. Some con artists will even keep you on the phone while they point you in the direction of a cryptocurrency ATM and walk you through the process of inserting cash and converting it to cryptocurrency. They'll give you a QR code to scan to send the cryptocurrency, and once you do, it will be sent directly to their digital wallet and vanish.

On job sites, con artists post bogus positions. They may even send unsolicited job offers for positions selling or mining cryptocurrencies, helping customers convert money to cryptocurrency, or assisting with investor recruitment. However, you can only begin these fictitious "jobs" if you pay a charge in cryptocurrency. It is consistently a swindle. These con artists offer you a check to deposit into your bank account as the first task of your "job." (That check will be a forgery.) They'll instruct you to take a portion of that money out, purchase cryptocurrency for a fictitious "customer," and send it to a cryptocurrency account they provide. However, if you do, the money will be lost, and you will be responsible for paying the bank back.

BLACKMAIL SCAMS

Scammers may contact you through email or United States mail, claiming to have compromising photographs, videos, or personal information about you. They'll threaten to reveal it unless you pay them in cryptocurrency. It's not a good idea. This is blackmail and attempted criminal extortion. Immediately inform the Police or FBI if this happens to you. Don't engage with the scammers, don't pay them, and don't provide any personal information. Delete the email or letter. If you have already paid, file a complaint with the Internet Crime Complaint Center (ICC).

FAKE WEBSITES

Bogus sites feature fake testimonials and crypto jargon promising massive, guaranteed returns, provided you keep investing or buying their services. They might even mimic a legitimate website or company to look natural. For example, a site may claim to be an exchange but is only designed to steal your login credentials so criminals can access your real account and take your money. Others might install cryptocurrency mining software on your device without you realizing it, using up processing power and driving up your energy bill while earning the fraudster's money.

PUMP-AND-DUMP SCHEMES

It's illegal for people or firms who own a significant amount of a particular stock or other assets to spread false information to drive down the price so they can buy more at a lower cost, then "pump" the price back up by sharing true information or selling their assets. These schemes frequently occur in the cryptocurrency marketplace. They often start with someone buying a large amount of one particular cryptocurrency, then hyping it on social media or online forums to get others to buy it, too, "pumping" up its price. When the price reaches a peak, the original owner quickly sells all their holdings, "dumping" them on the market and causing the price to crash for everyone else still holding that currency.

If you see posts online promising massive returns from investing in a particular cryptocurrency, be very wary—it could be part of a pump-and-dump scheme. And if you're considering investing in any digital asset, do your homework first and consult financial professionals to get advice tailored to your circumstances.

PONZI SCHEMES

Like pump-and-dump schemes, Ponzi schemes rely on convincing people to buy into a fraudulent investment to make money for the people running the scheme. But instead of using false information, Ponzi schemes promise guaranteed or highly high returns with little or no risk. They often claim that they will use your investment to trade cryptocurrency or conduct other activities to generate a profit, then share that profit with you. But in reality, there is usually no trading or other legitimate activity, and the people running the scheme simply use new investors' money to pay existing investors their "returns," giving the impression that everyone is making money.

Above are some of the most common cryptocurrency scams. But this is not an exhaustive list, and new scams are constantly popping up. The best way to protect yourself is to be aware of the risks and to exercise caution before investing in any digital asset.

CHAPTER 11

THE BEST CRYPTOCURRENCIES TO INVEST IN TODAY

If you're interested in investing in or trading cryptocurrencies, you must pick a good one to start with. Thousands of different coins are competing for your investment and attention, but not all will be worth your time.

The first thing you should know is that the world of cryptocurrency moves very fast, and this is more than just a fad. These currencies transform how we handle money, and keeping up with the latest trends is essential for success.

The one thing we find most important is never to invest in something you don't understand, which goes double for any cryptocurrency. This book will try and give you a brief glimpse into the world of cryptocurrency and introduce you to some coins that are making big waves right now.

We've got all the best information about how to invest in these coins and what makes them worth your time, but first, let's look at why they're becoming so popular.

BITCOIN (BTC)

Bitcoin is the king of cryptocurrencies, and it's not hard to see why. It was the first cryptocurrency created in 2009 but has remained #1 for many reasons.

The main reason why so many people are using Bitcoins is that they are simple to use. Transactions are quick, and even beginners can usually figure out how things work pretty fast. There are also no fees involved with these transactions because there is no need for a middleman (you will save money when making payments).

However, the most significant benefit is decentralization; nobody can interfere with your funds because any government or entity doesn't control Bitcoins. This makes the currency very secure, which accounts for its high value. You can also generate more Bitcoins if you have a powerful enough PC.

Finally, while Bitcoins are rising in value, their low production rate means they won't become too expensive to buy. It's probably best not to sit on these coins for too long because the market is highly volatile, and prices fluctuate quickly.

ETHEREUM (ETH)

The Ethereum blockchain is second only to Bitcoin regarding market share and value, making it very popular among investors and traders. The main reason why this cryptocurrency is so valuable is because of its smart contract features and ability to support an array of decentralized applications (or Dapps).

These smart contracts allow users to create different kinds of cryptocurrencies outside ETH. For example, if you wanted to create an ERC-20 token, you would need ETH.

Many Dapps have unique tokens for sale or use on the Ethereum blockchain. Because of this, Ethereum is worth more than its value as a cryptocurrency, and trading tokens built on the platform will make you even more money.

Ethereum takes decentralization very seriously because there's no single point of entry for your funds regarding security. This makes hacking attempts much less likely, although they are not impossible (which can be said about any kind of crypto). Users are kept safe by the platform's cryptographic encryption, which is essential in keeping things private and anonymous.

SOLANA (SOL)

Bitcoin may be the king of cryptocurrencies, but Solana is their prince. This coin has been rising in value very quickly over the past few months, and many believe it will only keep growing.

The reason why this cryptocurrency is so valuable right now is its speed. Solana transactions are complete in just a few seconds, while some currencies can take hours or even days! The main reason for this speed is Proof-of-History (PoH) which helps control consensus speeds compared to other blockchains.

Another benefit of this cryptocurrency is that it uses Proof-of-Stake (PoS), meaning that you won't have to wait around burning electricity when Solana is mining anymore. You will even get paid dividends from every transaction, and the only way to benefit from this coin is by actually using it.

Finally, because of the large user base, buying and selling Solana will be simple, even if you're a beginner. This can make things easier for those looking to get started as soon as possible (although always do your research before investing in any Coins).

FTX TOKEN (FTT)

The future of cryptocurrency is secure exchanges. There are many of these exchanges popping up out there. Still, they don't yet offer the security that they need to operate properly. Because of this, FTX Token was created with one goal: to make an exchange that is powerful enough to handle the demand of today's market.

Their platform will be scalable and handle a large volume of trades at any given point. This token also provides users with access to more than just currencies. Users can also trade commodities like oil, gas, gold, etc. They will even split payments for some transactions, so you won't have to pay extra fees or wait around for your money.

Another great feature about FTX is that its fee structure will be shallow. This means that the platform's cost will be much lower than most other exchanges when you add in their decentralization. Using this exchange becomes a reward for traders/investors instead of a chore.

FTX is backed by a strong team developing blockchain technology since 2010. They also boast the highest customer satisfaction in the industry, which will keep people returning to their platform. This can make getting FTX very simple, even if you're new to cryptocurrency.

CARDANO (ADA)

Cardano is another cryptocurrency that's been rising in value over the past couple of months. Much like Solana, this coin has risen quickly and now boasts one of the highest values on the market today. This rise in value is because Cardano makes transactions much cheaper than other coins.

For example, it costs just $0.01 to send ADA coins, which are converted automatically into gas depending on how much power you want to use when making your transfers. This means that no matter what you're transferring, whether it's fiat or crypto, it will be very cheap compared to almost any other exchange out there right now.

This token also has an excellent user interface, making buying/selling/trading cryptocurrencies more accessible than ever. This makes Cardano one of the best for new investors. However, it's essential to do your research before making any investments.

Another great thing about this coin is its open-source code that makes all transactions transparent to users. This can help reduce suspicious activity and limit fraud, enabling more people to use the currency safely and ensuring their personal information remains safe and secure.

Cardano uses a faster blockchain than most other currencies on the market today, so if you're looking for speed over efficiency, this may be the currency for you.

BINANCE COIN (BNB)

Binance Coin is one of the newest cryptocurrencies on the market today. It's only been around for less than a year. Still, this coin has already climbed to amazing heights. It is now one of the most valuable currencies on the market today. This coin boasts an incredible user interface, making buying/selling/trading cryptocurrencies more accessible than ever.

However, Binance Coin doesn't just have good looks; it also offers some compelling features that simplify your experience while using this platform and ensure that money transfers are fast without being too costly. For example, BNB users will get discounts when listing fees or trading large volumes. They'll even receive incentives when they trade their coins for other currencies or use them to invest in ICOs.

The last thing we want to mention about BNB is that it has a solid team behind it and has been designed by some of the best developers in the industry. This means you can count on the currency and know that it's not going anywhere anytime soon, which can attract more investors/traders and drastically improve your success rate as an investor/trader.

POLKADOT (DOT)

Polkadot is a token that has been around since 2017 but didn't launch until 2018. This token allows users to transfer money/assets/cryptocurrencies between blockchains and advantage of this platform's excellent features. This means you can seamlessly switch from Ethereum-based currencies to NEO; for example, you can switch between any currency hosted on the Polkadot blockchain.

One of the best things about this currency is that it's not limited to cryptocurrency transfers. You can also transfer fiat assets, smart contracts, and almost any other type of transfer you can imagine! This makes PolkaDot one of the most versatile currencies on this list, making it an excellent choice for anyone looking to diversify their portfolio or streamline their trading strategy.

Despite being relatively new, PolkaDot has amassed an impressive team behind it who have worked in some of the biggest companies in the world, including Microsoft, Google, and Apple. The currency has some great features, including feeless transfers, thanks to subchains linked to the main chain.

ALGORAND (ALGO)

Algorand is an entirely decentralized system that was first introduced to the public in 2017. This platform allows users to send and receive money globally without fear of downtime or tampering from outside parties, making it great for those who often trade or invest large amounts. It can even be used for payment by those who commonly use e-commerce websites online.

In addition, Algorand offers some compelling incentives to investors and traders, including 1% annual interest on deposits and an intriguing referral program that can earn you up to 15%

commissions per social media account! However, the best part about this currency is that it can process transactions within seconds or minutes – even if a million people are trying to do so simultaneously.

This means that those who use Algorand as a form of payment never have to worry about slow transactions or getting "stuck" in a long queue – which can be a massive pain for developers and e-commerce websites owners alike!

Since this is a new currency, it comes with all the benefits you'd expect from an early-stage investment, such as reasonable fees, free transfers, and decentralized blockchain technology. This allows users to reap the rewards without worrying about downtime or other problems that might come with transferring funds between platforms.

There are lots of cryptocurrencies out there, but these stand above the rest right now. They've been growing fast, and they look like they'll continue to grow well into the future. This means that these coins will be good investments for people looking to make money by buying them and then selling them at a higher value (or holding onto them long term). However, it's important to remember that not every cryptocurrency will grow, so only invest in what you can afford to lose.

CHAPTER 12

TIPS FOR INVESTING IN CRYPTOCURRENCY SAFELY.

All investments carry risk, but some experts consider cryptocurrency one of the riskier investment choices. These tips can help you make educated choices if you plan to invest in cryptocurrencies.

HAVE A STRATEGY FOR CRYPTO TRADING

Many sharks are eager to take your money, making it difficult to distinguish between legitimate bitcoin suggestions and frauds.

Take a step back from the frenzy when you're presented with much information about a cryptocurrency. Consider the platform or project critically. How many people utilize it? What issue does it address? Avoid currencies that make lofty promises but fail to deliver on them.

Before you invest, learn about cryptocurrency exchanges. It's estimated that there are over 500 exchanges to choose from. Do your research, read reviews, and talk with more experienced investors before moving forward.

KNOW HOW TO STORE YOUR DIGITAL CURRENCY

If you buy cryptocurrency, you have to store it. You can keep it on an exchange or in a digital wallet. While there are different wallets, each has its benefits, technical requirements, and security. As with exchanges, you should investigate your storage choices before investing.

Once you have chosen exchange and a wallet, take security measures. These might include two-factor authentication or using a biometric key. Also, know how to spot phishing attempts. Be wary of anyone who asks for personal information or login credentials.

DIVERSIFY YOUR INVESTMENTS

Diversification is key to any good investment strategy when investing in cryptocurrency. Don't put all your money in Bitcoin, for example, just because that's the name you know. There are thousands of options, and it's better to spread your investment across several currencies. This will protect you if the value of one falls sharply.

PREPARE FOR VOLATILITY

The cryptocurrency market is highly volatile, so be prepared for the ups and downs. You will see dramatic swings in prices. If your investment portfolio or mental well-being can't handle that, cryptocurrency might not be wise for you.

Cryptocurrency is all the rage right now, but remember, it is still in its relative infancy and is considered highly speculative. Investing in something new comes with challenges, so be prepared. If you plan to participate, do your research, and invest conservatively to start.

AVOID THE FEAR OF MISSING OUT.

With any new technology or investment opportunity, there is always the potential to miss out on something big. When it comes to cryptocurrency, this feeling can be amplified.

Don't let FOMO drive your investment decisions. Be patient and do your research before investing. You might never start if you wait for the perfect time to invest. No one knows where the market will go next, so don't get caught up in trying to predict the future. Instead, focus on making informed choices and diversifying your investments.

BUILD YOUR EMERGENCY FUND

Building an emergency fund should be a priority, according to financial advisors. This will help you survive if your investments lose value and give you time to recover from market fluctuations without taking out loans or credit cards. Make sure that the money is accessible and easy for you to withdraw because if there is ever an emergency, like sudden unemployment or medical expenses, you won't have time to wait for third-party reimbursement.

USE COLD STORAGE WALLETS.

Cold storage is keeping your cryptocurrency offline to protect it against security breaches. Hackers require access to your private key (a secret code) and online payment details before they can steal your virtual money, but if your funds are kept offline, they aren't available on the open market. To get access, a hacker would have to get both your private key and the password protecting the wallet on your computer or mobile device.

There are several ways you can create a cold storage wallet:

- Paper wallets - A paper wallet is an offline mechanism for storing your cryptocurrency that involves printing out a public address and private keys onto a piece of paper. This also has some apparent disadvantages regarding physical security - if someone finds your paper wallet, they could steal all of your money! It's therefore recommended that you engrave the keys on metal plates that will last longer but must be kept safe from prying eyes. You could also store multiple copies in secure locations such as bank vaults or safety deposit boxes.

- Hardware wallets - This is a physical, electronic device created to store cryptocurrency securely offline. It's often considered the safest cold storage option because it doesn't expose your private key to the internet - you can input your PIN to send payments but not withdraw any money from the wallet itself, which makes it nearly impossible to hack. Hardware wallets are generally waterproof and built with high durability in mind. They're also typically compatible with different cryptocurrencies, so your hardware wallet could still be used for future transactions if one digital currency becomes more popular. The major downside of this method is that you'll have to purchase a hardware wallet to store your cryptocurrency tokens on, so this isn't recommended if you only have a small amount to invest.

SECURE EXCHANGES

When choosing where to buy cryptocurrencies, it's essential to consider the security features offered by each exchange. A secure and transparent platform will state the fees and commissions that apply to each type of transaction, which you should aim to keep below 3 percent. For more significant transactions involving hundreds or thousands of dollars worth of cryptocurrency, you may also want to consider using a market with lower commission rates so that your money can go further.

Look out for exchanges that offer additional security features such as:

- Two-factor authentication - This security feature sends a separate confirmation code from your phone when you sign in via an app or website. It's considered one of the most effective ways to protect your accounts against hackers attempting to break into their systems because even if they manage to steal your password, it won't be enough on its own.
- Email alerts - you should set up email alerts so that you're notified when someone attempts to access your account, including password resets. This is another good security feature because if your session has been interrupted or someone tries to hack into your account, you'll get an instant notification.
- Cold storage options - The safest way to store cryptocurrency tokens offline is in cold wallets. Still, exchanges can also provide this service for users who aren't technically savvy enough to do it themselves. Make sure the exchange offers a multi-signature option - this requires more than one key before any transactions are accepted, so even the owner isn't able to run off with the money!

BE PATIENT

You should never rush when it comes to investing in cryptocurrency tokens because this greatly increases your chances of making a mistake and losing money. Take calculated risks and focus on diversifying your portfolio so that no single digital currency dominates over the others. That way, if something happens to one particular token, there'll be less impact on your entire investment.

A lot can happen in a short time when it comes to cryptocurrency, which is why you shouldn't take any unnecessary risks. It's also worth bearing in mind that after

Bitcoin started gaining traction with mainstream audiences, other cryptocurrencies began popping up in its wake - but not all of them will survive for very long! This rapid expansion means there's plenty more opportunity for growth, but it also means that there'll be a lot more competition from other investors trying to do the same thing.

DIVERSIFY YOUR INVESTMENTS

One of the most important things to remember when you're investing in funds is that there's no point in putting all your eggs into one basket. A diverse portfolio will include at least three or four types of cryptocurrency tokens so that if one drops, you'll still have another to rely on for future growth.

Different cryptocurrencies are designed with different purposes in mind, so they perform best under certain conditions, which vary from token to token. Some are better for trading, while others are more suitable for long-term investment because they take longer to gain momentum and tend to be less volatile once they've reached their peak. You should also consider how each digital currency compatibility with other cryptocurrencies too - some tokens may only work well when paired up with specific tokens, while others can be used to carry out transactions with every other cryptocurrency on the market.

Adding up all these different factors will make a big difference when you're putting together a portfolio because you won't have to rely on just one or two digital currencies for support if something goes wrong.

Using multiple exchanges is another way of diversifying your investments, particularly when dealing with more significant amounts of money, because it reduces your exposure to any security breaches. You should also try using more than one fiat currency so that your money isn't affected if something goes wrong with a particular currency or if there's an international exchange rate issue. For example, Japan has been leading the charge in terms of trading volume for Bitcoin, so it might be a good idea to keep some of your money in USD if you're focusing on the American market.

These tips can help you make educated choices if you plan to invest in cryptocurrencies.

CHAPTER 13

CRYPTOCURRENCY EXCHANGES AND BROKERS

A cryptocurrency exchange is where you would buy or sell cryptocurrencies. It is like the stock market in that they are a place to connect buyers and sellers.

They can offer lower fees than brokerages but will lack exposure compared to brokers. If you have no experience with trading or exchanges, this might be for you since there are fewer chances of being scammed here due to buyer-seller protection. Brokers often require access to your bank account, while an exchange does not need your personal information. However, many prefer brokers because they seem "safer" because of their connection with traditional banking institutions. You can get started on Coinbase.

WHAT IS A CRYPTOCURRENCY BROKER?

Cryptocurrency brokers are websites that allow you to buy cryptocurrencies with fiat money, like US dollars. While there is no real broker-dealer relationship between the customer and the exchange, most cryptocurrency exchanges have generally accepted rules of conduct for their platforms. If customers do not follow these guidelines or violate them through unlawful acts such as hacking into other people's accounts, they can be banned from using the platform.

A cryptocurrency broker allows consumers to buy and sell cryptocurrencies using the internet. A broker charges users premiums for utilizing the platform for this service.

SUITABLE FOR BEGINNERS

Cryptocurrency brokers provide the ideal climate for those new to cryptocurrency trading and those who wish to buy Bitcoin, Litecoin, Ethereum, or other cryptocurrencies. The buyer and vendor deal with the broker platform when exchanging fiat currencies for cryptocurrencies and vice versa.

Users may benefit from buying and selling cryptocurrencies through a broker in various ways: they can purchase and sell cryptocurrencies at the behest of the broker. A cryptocurrency broker is also helpful if you only want to acquire a small number of coins.

Users can directly exchange fiat currencies like €, CHF, GBP, and USD for Bitcoin, Ethereum, Litecoin, and other digital currencies.

Simply create an account by entering your email address and validating it, then select from various payment options to deposit fiat currency. Once you've completed this process, you may start buying and selling digital assets.

A VAST RANGE OF SERVICES

Cryptocurrency brokers may also offer the service of keeping cryptocurrencies for their customers in facilitating trades. It also encourages users to entrust their bitcoins to a third-party wallet by allowing them to buy and sell cryptos straight from their Trezor and Ledger hardware wallets, thus enhancing user confidence.

When deciding which crypto broker to use, you should ensure that it has the skills to back up its claims. Your financial services provider should have cutting-edge security systems and meet current national regulatory standards. You want to be able to access your crypto broker platform 24 hours a day, 7 days a week, both via a desktop and mobile app.

CRYPTOCURRENCY EXCHANGE

Cryptocurrency exchanges operate like most online eCommerce marketplaces and portals such as eBay, Amazon, etc. The main difference with an actual stock market is that they do not have physical locations where customers can place orders for buying and selling. Instead, these businesses depend on telecoms and computer networks (like the Internet) to conduct business transactions between buyers and sellers who wish to trade cryptocurrencies via different orders, such as limit orders, stop-loss orders, etc., just like any other type of commodity trading transaction. Cryptocurrencies can therefore be bought at current prices using fiat money from your bank account or debit card, which you can transfer to the exchange's wallet address.

If you want to trade cryptocurrencies directly with other buyers and sellers, you might want to investigate using a cryptocurrency exchange. In contrast to a crypto broker, a cryptocurrency exchange is an online platform for traders of cryptocurrencies for other digital currencies or fiat currencies that do not involve a broker, depending on current market rates. As a result, the transaction of fiat currencies and cryptocurrencies happens immediately between buyers and sellers via the exchange operator's platform.

Cryptocurrency exchanges are ideal platforms for more experienced bitcoin holders and traders who wish to take advantage of price changes through speculation to make profits and avoid losses.

REGULATION AND COMPLIANCE

As always, ensure you're protecting yourself against scams and money laundering, both common phenomena in cryptocurrency. Remember that a fully transparent and compliant cryptocurrency exchange will likely prioritize providing users with dependable access to its platform and utilizing state-of-the-art security techniques.

Cryptocurrency exchanges and brokers allow you to buy and sell cryptocurrencies. There are some significant differences between the two:

For example, on an exchange like Coinbase Pro or Kraken, cryptocurrency can be purchased with fiat currency (e.g., USD). On a broker site such as Coinmama, you cannot—it is strictly for purchasing cryptocurrency with another form of virtual currency. One advantage that both have in common? Before starting on either platform, you don't need prior experience buying digital assets!

WHY WOULD I USE A BROKER OVER AN EXCHANGE?

The main benefit of using a crypto broker is that they provide quick liquidity by allowing users to purchase large amounts without waiting several days for bank transfers/payments processing. However, they are often more expensive than exchanges.

WHY WOULD I USE AN EXCHANGE OVER A BROKER?

Exchanges tend to have lower fees because you do not need to pay for the service of converting your fiat currency into cryptocurrency (i.e., linking your bank account). Plus, some exchanges allow users to purchase cryptocurrencies with credit or debit cards—the latter can be done on Coinmama! Be careful, though: It's common knowledge that if you own less than $70 worth of cryptocurrency and decide to buy it using a credit card at Coinbase Pro, you will incur high-interest rates (around 20%). If you want to avoid paying such sky-high interest rates, look elsewhere for brokerage services like Coinmama. Exchanges also tend to have a wider variety of cryptocurrencies available, but they can be more difficult for beginners.

WHAT IS THE BEST EXCHANGE?

There isn't one! Each has its pros and cons depending on what you are looking for—there is no "best cryptocurrency broker or exchange." In general, Coinbase Pro tends to attract less experienced users who wish to purchase large amounts of crypto without spending too much time learning about the process, while exchanges like Binance draw in traders due to their low fees and many trading pairs with different currencies

Once you have set up a wallet, you can use your public address to receive money and send money to others. You can also purchase or trade Litecoin and Bitcoin on exchanges like Binance and Coinbase Pro (part of GDAX).

CHAPTER 14

STRATEGIES FOR INVESTING IN CRYPTOCURRENCIES

There are several strategies that you can adopt when investing in cryptocurrencies. Let's go through them one at a time.

1) BUY AND HOLD

Buying and holding is the most straightforward strategy here. You put in money, buy a cryptocurrency or multiple cryptos, hold on to it for a couple of months/years until their value increases, then cash out. Yes, everything would have been much easier if you had bought bitcoin 10 years ago when it was cheap(er), but hey - better late than never! So what do you need to do? Just buy high-quality coins with potential for appreciation and keep an eye on the news now and then so that you're aware of any significant changes in the coin's value.

2) BUY AND HOLD WITH MARGIN TRADING (ADVANCED)

This strategy is for people willing to put in extra effort/time for better returns. The idea here is that you buy the same coin, but instead of holding all of them, you have only 10% or 20% of it at any given time. You then sell another portion of your holdings on margin(borrowed money), which means using the loaned money to buy more coins, so now you have 30%/40%/50%. Continue this until you have cashed out your original 100%. Rinse & Repeat if necessary. This requires some capital as well as a bit of trading knowledge beforehand. If you don't have either at the moment but want to try this strategy, you can join a trading pool. You put money together with others (and get assigned someone to trade on your behalf if necessary) and share profits.

3) ICO INVESTMENT

ICO stands for Initial Coin Offering. It's like an IPO. It usually happens at the beginning of a project when there is almost no user base or market value/appreciation. An ICO is generally announced on BTC forums. People interested in investing send their contributions to ETH, BTC, or whatever cryptocurrency they choose. The company then distributes the tokens at a certain ratio(e.g., 1 ETH = 1000 XYZ tokens). People who buy during an ico will likely want to hold on to their tokens and sell them off later when the value increases, so they might not be as active in trading as those who bought and held.

4) EXCHANGE PLATFORM TRADING

This strategy is for the more advanced traders. Cryptocurrency exchanges are platforms where people buy, sell, and trade crypto coins. Some popular examples of these exchanges are Binance, Poloniex, Bittrex, etc. I won't go into depth about how to use them here but will quickly explain this trading strategy you can adopt on such exchanges. Say you want to buy ADA (a cryptocurrency).

5) ARBITRAGE TRADING

Arbitrage is taking advantage of differences in market prices across different exchanges for buying/selling cryptocurrencies so that you can profit from them. This strategy requires technical knowledge, time, and effort to set up an automated bot or script that will do all the work for you. You then need to keep an eye on things, check any significant changes in price levels across exchanges (coinbase vs. gdax, etc.), and manually intervene when conditions become favorable for arbing.

6) STAKING COINS

This is a rather special strategy because you're not trading with the coins per see, but instead using them for their intended purpose. Some cryptocurrencies need to be "locked" in wallets for specific periods (from hours to days/weeks/months), and you'll get rewarded proportionally based on how long you locked up to your funds. Mathematically this is similar (but better!) to buying & holding - say it's like investing $100 now and getting back $120 in 2 years. However, there are some key differences - first, that initial amount you invested will be locked away, so if BTC crashes during that period, you won't lose money at all; second, even if the price of the coin goes down, you'll still get your share of the original amount, so this strategy is better than just holding. The only thing to remember is that some coins might have a cap on how much money can be locked away (e.g., 1% of the total supply). If you're looking for such opportunities, check out bitshares, NEO and COSS.

7) MARGIN TRADING/LENDING

This is similar to Exchange Platform Trading - where you lend someone BTC or ETH by making a margin trade order. Still, instead of doing it manually, like in more straightforward exchanges, your funds will automatically be lent out and re-invested when conditions are favorable. The difference here is that the profits do not belong to you - they will go to the platform provider instead. The risks are pretty high here, too - you could lose all your money if the price of ETH/BTC drops to $0!

8) DIVIDEND COINS

This is quite similar to staking coins, but not quite. Even though some coins(e.g., NEO) claim that they offer dividends for holding their tokens, this isn't profitable or worth it in any way as a strategy because the amounts they give back per token are far below the amount you could have earned just by buying & holding(and selling off later). However, specific cryptocurrencies will give out more than just one token's worth of dividend per unit - these are usually ICOs that have been successful enough to generate lots of dividends.

9) BOUNTY/AIRDROP COINS

You can collect these coins simply by holding BTC or ETH in your wallet or completing small tasks like following them on Twitter, etc. Generally, the idea is to promote awareness, so it's not really intended as a long-term strategy - but if you're collecting coins for fun anyway, you might as well cash them in when they hit an exchange.

10) PASSIVE INCOME STRATEGY (BORROWING AGAINST CRYPTO-ASSETS)

This one requires some technical knowledge about how Ethereum smart contracts work, and I'll focus more on this later... Most readers won't be interested in this one because it's rather complex and requires much technical know-how. However, I include it here because there is a way to get 'free' BTC/LTC by using your altcoins, and there are people actively doing this right now!

CHAPTER 15

THE BENEFIT AND COMMON MISTAKE OF PEOPLE INVESTING IN CRYPTO

THE BENEFITS OF CRYPTOCURRENCIES

Cryptocurrencies offer several benefits over traditional fiat currencies. They are swift and efficient to transact, global and borderless, and highly secure. Cryptocurrencies also have the potential to disrupt traditional financial institutions and create new economic opportunities for people around the world. Below are just a few of the many benefits of cryptocurrencies.

EASY TRANSACTIONS

Crypto transactions can be made quickly, at low cost, and in a manner more private than most other transactions. Using a simple smartphone app, hardware wallet, or exchange wallet, anyone can send and receive a variety of cryptocurrencies.

Some types of cryptocurrencies, including Bitcoin, Litecoin, and Ethereum, can be bought with cash at a Bitcoin ATM. A bank account isn't always required to use crypto. Someone could buy bitcoin at an ATM using cash and then send those coins to their phone. For people who lack access to the traditional financial system, this may be one of the biggest pros of cryptocurrency.

INCREDIBLE SECURITY

Because they are based on cryptography and blockchain security, decentralized cryptocurrencies tend to make for secure forms of payment. This might be one of the most certain benefits of cryptocurrency.

Crypto security is determined in large part by hash rate. The higher the hash rate, the more computing power it would take to compromise the network. Bitcoin is the most secure cryptocurrency, with the highest hash rate of any network.

However, using a crypto exchange is only as secure as the exchange itself. Most incidents of crypto being hacked involve exchanges being hacked or individuals making mistakes.

SHORT SETTLEMENT TIMES AND LOW FEES

While some people only want to invest in cryptocurrency for price appreciation, others might benefit from using crypto as a medium of exchange.

Bitcoin and Ether transactions could cost anywhere from nickels and dimes to several dollars or more. Other cryptocurrencies like Litecoin, XRP, and others can be sent for pennies or less. Payments for most cryptos settle in seconds or minutes. Wire transfers at banks can cost significantly more and often take three to five business days to settle.

EXPONENTIAL INDUSTRY GROWTH

The cryptocurrency industry has been one of the fastest-growing markets that most of us have seen. Being involved now might reasonably be compared to being involved with companies on the leading edge of the internet back in the 1990s and early 2000s.

OUTSIZED RETURNS

It's no secret that Bitcoin has been the best-performing asset of the last 12 years. When it began in 2009, Bitcoin essentially had no value. In the following years, it would rise to a fraction of a penny and eventually to tens of thousands of dollars. This represents millions of percentage points' worth of gains. By comparison, the S&P 500 index of stocks returns an average of about 8% per year.

Some altcoins have outperformed Bitcoin by wide margins at times, although many of those later saw their prices collapse. Gains like these might be among the most well-known cryptocurrency benefits.

Volatility has characterized prices in the crypto space, which has been one of the critical benefits of cryptocurrency for day traders and speculators.

MORE PRIVATE TRANSACTIONS

Privacy can be one of the benefits of cryptocurrency, but crypto isn't as private as some might think. Blockchains create a public ledger that records all transactions forever. While this ledger only shows wallet addresses, tracking transactions becomes possible if an observer can connect a user's identity to a specific wallet.

While it's worth noting that most crypto transactions are pseudonymous, there are ways to make more anonymous transactions. Coin mixing services group transactions, making it hard to pick them apart from one another and confusing outside observers. Individuals who run a full node also make their transactions more opaque because observers can't always tell if the transactions running through the node were sent by the person running the node or by someone else.

Methods like these are for more advanced users and could prove difficult for those new to crypto.

PORTFOLIO DIVERSIFICATION

Cryptocurrency has become known as a non-correlated asset class. Crypto markets essentially function independently of other markets, and their price action tends to be determined by factors other than those affecting stocks, bonds, and commodities.

Any asset that has risen by millions of percentage points over just twelve years, as several crypto coins have, clearly is not correlated to anything else. But it's worth noting that during the last few years, cryptos have begun to sometimes trade in tandem with stocks for short periods.

INFLATION HEDGE

Mineable cryptocurrencies with a limited supply cap, like Bitcoin, Litecoin, and Monero, to name a few, are thought to be good hedges against inflation. Because monetary inflation can occur when central banks and governments print more money, increasing the supply, more scarce things tend to appreciate.

With more and more new dollars chasing fewer and fewer coins, the price of these fixed-supply coins, as measured in dollars, has a higher chance of going up. Additionally, the Bitcoin protocol, for example, is designed to keep those coins scarce regardless of what happens with monetary policy.

CROSS-BORDER PAYMENTS

Cryptocurrencies have no regard for national borders. An individual in one country can send coins to someone in a different country without difficulty. With traditional financial services, getting funds across international borders can take a long time and come with hefty fees. In some cases, doing so might be impossible due to regulations, sanctions, or tensions between specific countries.

A MORE INCLUSIVE FINANCIAL SYSTEM

Some of the benefits of cryptocurrency extend to people who don't have access to the traditional financial system. Due to its decentralized and permission-less nature, one of the benefits of cryptocurrency is that anyone can participate.

People don't have any financial authority or government permission to use the crypto ecosystem. (Though it's worth noting that Bitcoin *mining* is banned in China.) They also don't necessarily need to have a bank account. There are billions of people today who are "unbanked," meaning they have no access to the financial system, including bank accounts. With crypto, all these people need is a smartphone, which can become their bank.

TRANSACTIONAL FREEDOM

One of the great benefits of crypto is that it can be used to exchange value between two parties. This can be done independently of any third party, making the transaction more accessible and censorship-resistant.

Banks or other payment processors can choose to cut off services to anyone for any reason. This can make things difficult for some journalists, political dissidents, or other individuals working in nations with oppressive government regimes. Because no central authority governs Bitcoin or most other cryptocurrencies, it's tough to stop anyone from using them.

24/7 MARKETS

In the case of the New York Stock Exchange (NYSE), stock markets are only open on weekdays during the regular business hours of 9:30 am to 4:30 pm Eastern Time. Most traditional financial markets are not open for business during nights, weekends, and holidays.

On the other hand, crypto markets trade 24 hours a day, seven days a week, without exception. Some of the only things that could interrupt a person's ability to trade cryptocurrency would be a power outage, internet outage, or centralized exchange outage.

DECENTRALIZE

A decentralized cryptocurrency's structure does not rely on a single computer or server, which would fail if a hacker gained access. Instead, it depends on many computers to keep the trusted record, known as the blockchain. These records are updated in multiple locations when transactions are made, so the others will have accurate copies when one is hacked or forged.

No one entity or group has complete control. Decentralization is often built into cryptocurrencies based on a distributed ledger known as the blockchain. This records every transaction made, with each participant's digital signature attached to it. These blocks are updated in real-time across the whole network so everyone can access them anytime.

When someone decides to make a cryptocurrency decentralized, there can be no central control or issuing authority for the currency. Decisions about how the currency operates are ratified by consensus among participants in the network, and other nodes must validate transactions on that network before they are accepted as true. The benefit of decentralizing currency is that because there isn't one central point of failure that would allow an attacker to bring down or corrupt the system, any damage to the network is unlikely to affect any of its users.

ELIMINATES INFLATION

Some cryptocurrencies are finite in supply, meaning a maximum number of coins will ever be in circulation. Others do not have a maximum cap but limit the number of new coins generated yearly. This limits inflation, as the coins will never be devalued because of an increase in supply. For example, as of December 2017, the number of Bitcoins that can exist capped at 21 million tokens.

Some cryptos, such as Ripple and IOTA, don't have a maximum cap. Instead, they use dynamic pricing to manage token distribution to ensure they are fairly distributed and not hoarded by early adopters.

This method is even more effective than capped supply cryptos because it eliminates inflation, so there is never any excess currency that reduces the token's value.

DECENTRALIZED APPLICATIONS (DAPPS)

Contracts between two or more parties are often complicated and expensive by third-party processing services like banking institutions, governments, attorneys, brokers, exchanges, and others. These intermediaries create delays in transactions as they handle them on behalf of their clients. They also charge fees for their service of holding your money until you release it to someone else. Cryptocurrencies eliminate these fees because they operate using a distributed ledger system instead of a central authority to maintain control over the network and its currency. This means cryptocurrency transactions don't require personal information, which shields users from identity theft and reduces the chances of fraud.

Many users run a decentralized application (or Dapp) on a P2P(peer-to-peer) network with trustless protocols instead of a single server. Unlike an application centrally running, dapps are open source and operate autonomously.

This means dapps aren't served by one central computer but instead use blockchain technology to deliver their services without any centralized party involved. Instead of relying on data being processed and stored through servers owned by corporations or governments, all info is distributed across the network, so no one entity controls it. Dapps utilize smart contracts, which work similarly to legal contracts between two parties. These programs are run by the network and managed autonomously instead of controlled by a central party.

This means that Dapps remove third parties from the equation to provide services for users without them having to trust an unknown server host. This keeps costs down because there are no middlemen involved in transactions between users, so there's nowhere else their money can be taken when they pay for something online without any additional fees. Smart contracts guarantee payments to the seller once goods arrive at their destination. Hence, both parties know exactly when to expect delivery of goods or completion of work based on proof-of-work (PoW) algorithms that run throughout the network.

CHEAPER FEES THAN TRADITIONAL PAYMENT METHODS

When you make a transaction with your credit card or online bank account, fees are often involved, which go partly to intermediaries like Visa or PayPal. Networks built on blockchains don't need intermediaries to validate transactions, so fees are much lower when you use cryptos like Bitcoin.

For example, no third-party authority is involved when two parties make a transaction using Bitcoin. This means no one can freeze associated accounts or require additional documentation if they suspect fraudulent activity. It also saves them from having to pay credit card company charges. Cryptocurrencies have been around for quite some time and even experienced a severe spike in popularity back in late 2017/early 2018 because of increased mainstream exposure and media attention surrounding high profits for early holders. However, the fact that it's still somewhat new makes it risky as a long-term investment option due to its lack of wide-scale adoption and general understanding surrounding it/its usage. This is a risk that should be seriously considered when deciding whether or not to invest in a cryptocurrency.

As more and more people start using cryptos, so will the number of businesses accepting them as an option for payment. Like any other currency, cryptos can be exchanged for products and services within different industries, online marketplaces, and retail outlets worldwide.

IT CAN'T BE COUNTERFEITED.

Every piece of data stored on a blockchain has been irrevocably encrypted from its inception. Cryptographic functions ensure that only those who have been authorized to access the information can obtain it without needing to hack into a system first because all activities are monitored by everyone operating on the network at all times.

This means that instead of relying on a third party to keep a record of transactions and ensure that only the owner is spending the money, you can do it yourself without needing anyone's help. This eliminates the risk of counterfeit money being used because every existing unit has already been accounted for. Even some cryptocurrencies like zCash use zero-knowledge proofs, so transacting parties don't need to reveal their identities during the transaction process if they prefer not to do so.

TRANSFERABILITY

Cryptocurrencies are designed with one thing in mind: speed. Transactions made using cryptocurrency take place almost instantly, making them more competitive than other currently available methods. It also holds many advantages over bank transfers since they aren't bound by weekends, time zones, or national holidays.

You can send somebody Bitcoins in Canada, and they'll receive them the same day in Japan. Even cross-border transactions are faster with cryptos because you don't have to wait for banks to verify transfers when using decentralized networks instead of third-party services. Traditional wire transfers often take days to complete the transaction process without incurring high fees along the way.

With cryptocurrencies, all you need is a public key address which you can also share online with anyone who wants to make a payment. Sometimes this account will be managed by a digital wallet app that lets you store your tokens, but other options are available, too, depending on what kind of money is being exchanged.

If you have a business that accepts cryptos as a form of payment, you can save time and money instead of waiting for payments from customers who prefer to pay with them. Businesses can accept a wide range of tokens as valid payments and immediately exchange them for other digital or fiat currencies, so they never have to worry about holding their value.

A public key address is simply your account number on the blockchain. It allows others to send you crypto coins so you can keep track of your transactions and see how much money is in your wallet. Cryptocurrency wallets aren't like accounts where you store fiat currency at traditional banks because these virtual wallets allow you to buy, sell, spend, and trade cryptocurrencies.

With this type of account, there's no need to provide personal details or identity verification if you don't want to. All you need is the money in your wallet, and that's it. This makes them very secure because all transactions can be carried out anonymously without anyone needing to know who the sender was unless they provided their name when creating their wallet.

CAPITAL APPRECIATION

Also known as capital gains, refers to the increase of an investment's value from the amount invested. In cryptocurrency, this is when fiat currency or Bitcoin is bought with the assumption that it will be sold at a higher price in the future because its value has appreciated since it was obtained for a lower price earlier.

This contributes to significant growth in price and can lead to people making money off their investments in various cryptocurrencies. Capital appreciation is one of the main reasons so many people are interested in obtaining digital tokens because there's no telling how much they could be worth later on, even if they might not hold their value forever.

The market cap of cryptocurrencies gives us an idea of how much money there is available across all kinds of different tokens so we can quickly determine which ones have recently seen the most significant price rise. This number applies to the market's entire supply of cryptocurrencies and is constantly changing as money comes into play or leaves an asset, depending on what happens within the community.

For some cryptos like Bitcoin, there will only ever be 21 million tokens available for public consumption at any given time. Other currencies can have more than this amount in circulation, while others might even reach zero if they end up being completely abandoned by their creators. Hence, capital appreciation becomes rather difficult with these types of assets.

One interesting thing about holding certain digital currencies is that they could become more valuable over time, so people are inclined to hold onto them instead of spending them immediately, even if it doesn't help their wealth grow larger immediately. There are many reasons why someone might not be able to sell their tokens at the moment, which could either mean that there's no market for them or that merchants do not accept them as a valid form of payment.

Comparing bitcoin to the USD, the value of BTC is going up very quickly. If you had a million dollars before 2017 and a million after 2017, your USD would be worth the same, but your bitcoin would be worth over 3 million dollars.

THIN MARKETS

Thin markets are where financial exchanges take place but with few buyers and sellers. This makes it possible for people to purchase large quantities of currencies without significantly driving up the price because there aren't enough people interested in buying.

This can be hard on coin holders who want to make capital appreciation happen quickly because thin markets don't usually rise much in value over regular price points until more money appears within the community, causing prices to skyrocket. It also means that traders can buy low before things heat up and sell high once a substantial amount of people start investing.

Once the tide turns, the markets will become far more active as patterns begin to emerge, indicating a strong interest in certain coins from investors trying to buy as much as they can before everyone else does. This is why it's important to analyze trade volume for cryptocurrencies regularly because it provides clues about where money might start flowing next, so you don't miss out on an opportunity to sell at a premium price or buy low while things are still quiet.

HUGE GROWTH POTENTIAL

Cryptocurrency was the biggest story of 2017, generating much interest in the mainstream. This led to a massive price increase over time, resulting in capital appreciation for all investors. This has also prompted more people to buy altcoins as investments because they want their piece of the pie regarding the vast potential for profits across the board.

Most people are only familiar with Bitcoin as the most valuable cryptocurrency because of its market dominance over time. Still, there are thousands of other tokens out there which have seen significant price gains already. The world's leading currency is also the biggest one, followed by Ethereum and then XRP, with fourth place going to Bitcoin Cash.

Many different factors contribute to the growth in cryptocurrency prices over time. The most important thing to remember about these types of assets is that they're much more volatile than traditional currencies, which means price fluctuations will happen regularly, almost no matter what happens within the community at any given time.

Capital appreciation can come in all forms because there's much money in play, causing prices to rise or fall depending on how everyone else feels about holding or selling their coins. This volatility makes huge gains up and down possible while also making it risky because people might lose everything if things go south quickly.

It's easy to get caught up in day trading when you have access to many different exchanges where you can sell, buy or make more of the digital tokens you own over time. It's possible to generate significant profits by trying to capitalize on market conditions based on social media sentiment, news headlines, and political events that could influence people's views on cryptocurrency across the board.

COMMON CRYPTO MISTAKES

It's straightforward to become engrossed in the excitement of news headlines. We've included a few of the shockingly frequent crypto errors here.

BUYING JUST BECAUSE THE PRICE IS LOW

Cheap costs are not always a sign of a good deal. Prices can be intentionally low on occasion. Be wary of cryptocurrencies that have declining user rates. Additionally, developers frequently abandon projects, preventing them from being correctly updated and leaving the coin vulnerable to security threats.

Investing solely based on price is a common mistake made by beginner investors. Just because the price of a coin is low doesn’t mean it’s a good deal. Prices can be intentionally manipulated to look like a bargain. For example, during an altcoin season, you might see coins with declining user rates being offered at a discount. However, their developers often leave these coins abandoned, leaving them vulnerable to security threats.

GOING ‘ALL-IN.’

Some riskier trading platforms advise you to maximize your funds by placing as many bets as possible. This is a direct route to poverty.

Better cryptocurrency investment advice would be to retain an emergency cash reserve in an accessible savings account that is never invested in the market and to only spend a percentage of your capital—say, 5%—on high-risk investments. This will protect you from making rash decisions during a market crash and ensure that you always have some cash on hand in case of an emergency.

It's never a good idea to go "all-in" on any investment, but this is especially true for cryptocurrency. Some riskier trading platforms will even advise you to do this to maximize your profits. However, all this will put you on the fast track to poverty. A much wiser strategy would be to retain an emergency cash reserve in an accessible savings account that is never invested in the market. This way, you'll always have some cash on hand in case of an emergency. Additionally, you should only invest a percentage of your total capital—say, five percent—in high-risk investments. This will protect you from rash decisions during a market crash and ensure you don't lose everything if your gamble doesn't pay off.

THINKING CRYPTO IS 'EASY MONEY.

Making money through trading any form of financial instrument, including stocks, shares, or commodities like silver and gold, is not simple. The same is true of cryptocurrencies.

Anyone claiming otherwise is attempting to deceive you into making bad crypto decisions. "Easy money" schemes like these are often Ponzi schemes in disguise, so be careful before handing over any money.

Don't fall for the false promise of "easy money." Making money through trading any form of financial instrument, including stocks, shares, or commodities like silver and gold, is not simple. The same is true of cryptocurrencies. Anyone who tells you otherwise is probably trying to trick you into making some bad crypto decisions. "Easy money" schemes like these are often Ponzi schemes in disguise, so be very careful before handing over any of your hard-earned cash.

FORGETTING YOUR CRYPTO KEYPHRASE

Forgetting your crucial word is equivalent to misplacing the keys to a bank vault if you use a hardware wallet to store your cryptocurrency offline. All of your cryptos will be lost without your keyphrase.

Be sure to write down your keyphrase and store it in a safe place. Some people even store their keyphrase in multiple locations to be extra safe.

One of the worst things that can happen to a crypto investor is forgetting their crucial phrase. If you use a hardware wallet to store your cryptocurrency offline, forgetting your important phrase is equivalent to misplacing the keys in a bank vault. All of your cryptos will be lost without it. That's why it's essential to write down your key phrase and store it safely. Some people even store their key phrases in multiple locations to be extra safe.

CHAPTER 16

BITCOIN VS. THE DOLLAR

Bitcoin has a finite quantity of 21 million coins and will never be increased. In contrast, the United States government is constantly creating new money to increase its expanding debt. The first and most crucial difference is that Bitcoin cannot be deflated. Because of this, other currencies might inflate endlessly, while Bitcoin does not. It also implies that central banks and governments control other currencies, but it keeps control of its users across the world. There will only ever be 21 million bitcoins in circulation, and they cannot be taken from you if you secure them safely in your wallet. They do not rely on passing them through a bank or similar financial institution to keep your money safe; it's yours wholly and alone safeguarded on your computer with no third-party having access to it.

To give more context to the finite amount of bitcoins available, each block has an arbitrary number assigned to it that acts as a reference. The latest information shows there are about 12 million blocks with 25 bitcoins. 21 million divided by 12 million = 1.7 million left to mine before all the coins have been mined. Once this is done, people will still be able to gain access using their coin wallets, but no new ones will ever be created again. This makes bitcoin different than other fiat money that can be printed endlessly while devaluing existing cash and further raising prices for goods/services; this process is called inflation.

When you ask people the value of a single Bitcoin, the general response is, "it's worth what somebody will pay for it." It's true that the price of one Bitcoin has swung widely over time and was as low as $0.07 in 2011 and as high as $1,200 in late 2013. This dynamic pricing is due to its tiny market size (that is - there are not many Bitcoins traded at any given moment). Unlike most currencies, there simply aren't trillions of dollars worth of Bitcoin trading hands each day—for comparison, around $4 trillion worth of U.S. dollars are traded daily.

While that number explains some volatility, it doesn't explain nearly all. To do so, we need to look at speculative bubbles. To get a good picture of how extreme Bitcoin's price can swing, consider that following the Dot-Com bubble, the Dow Jones lost around 70% of its value.

Many argue that Cryptocurrencies are not real because they have no inherent value. Most official currencies today back themselves with some tangible resource (fiat money). For example, U.S. paper currency is officially "backed by the full faith and credit of the United States Government." Since Cryptocurrencies lack government backing, some see them as intrinsically worthless—or even worse than useless since they're giving people false hope for a free lunch, according to economists like Robert Shiller.

To understand if someone is justified in investing in cryptocurrency, you need to understand how it's different from traditional currencies.

First, Cryptocurrencies are decentralized—meaning, unlike fiat money, any central bank doesn't control them. They are an "open source" payment network telling anyone can contribute to the network or build applications on top of it (like building a website for money management). This is in stark contrast to every other form of money, which has a central authority that manages what gets added to the ledger and who can access it. The control over the system makes sense, given that centralized systems have worked well for thousands of years—but it also gives them their inherent value. After all, if you use someone else's money, it should be worth something because your counterparty risks not transferring it to you.

Second, cryptocurrencies are programmable - meaning developers can build applications on top of them (like money management systems). This opens up a world of possibilities for features like smart contracts and multi-signature wallets, which keep spending under control without involving a third party. While that might not be interesting to people who just want an alternative to their bank's debit card, businesses can benefit from keeping their ledgers and ultimately profits in-house instead of paying fees to use someone else's system.

Third, Cryptocurrencies are divisible—meaning each unit is subdivisible by all the other units (the smallest division is one hundred millionth of a single bitcoin). A little-known fact about fiat currencies is that they aren't divisible by all their subunits. For example, the Euro is divisible by 1,000,000 but not by 100. Why would that matter? Well, it means you can't buy something that costs 0.0001 Euros because there's no way to break up a Euro into smaller subunits (this might not seem like a big deal—but wait until you hear how much they make off your microtransactions).

Fourth, there is very little friction involved in transferring cryptocurrencies between individuals—meaning, unlike fiat money, it is relatively cheap and easy to transfer Bitcoins or Litecoins with anybody else who has an internet connection (and since the network is decentralized, this transaction happens directly between peers without involving intermediaries like banks). While this might not matter to each transaction, it can add up if you're doing several small transactions over a day—

and it also means there is no "bank run" risk where people rush to cash out their accounts simultaneously.

Fifth, Cryptocurrencies have incredibly low transaction costs—since they are decentralized and don't rely on banks or governments to manage them. While most currencies are accepted at multiple stores during an average week, most bank debit cards are only accepted in a single store or two (depending on the card type). This limits how much people have available for spending at any moment, limiting how much money circulates through the economy.

Sixth, cryptocurrencies come with built-in deflation—the opposite of inflation (when prices rise and your money becomes worthless). While most traditional currencies like the Euro or US dollars experience some deflation at any given moment, in the long run, they usually lose value due to inflation which means they constantly need to be reprinted. This is because governments monopolize printing money and often abuse it (sometimes using it to finance wars).

Unlike government-issued fiat money, cryptocurrencies aren't printed in unlimited quantities by central authorities. Instead, new units are mined into existence through a process known as "Proof of Work," where computers race against each other to solve computationally expensive problems that become progressively harder over time. As more Bitcoins are mined into existence, their value rises since they are harder to acquire—which encourages people to spend them, creating a virtuous cycle.

The main drawback of deflationary currencies is that they encourage hoarding, limiting the amount of money available for spending. This can somewhat inhibit economic growth because businesses can't always find customers with enough money to buy their goods (although this effect may be offset by the lower transaction costs that come with using cryptocurrencies).

THE DISTINCTION BETWEEN INFLATIONARY FIAT AND DEFLATIONARY DIGITAL STORE OF VALUE

The idea of deflating the money supply to spiraling combat inflation is not new, even in fiat currencies. The central banks have been doing it for decades now in developed economies, but only in recent times has deflation become an actual risk due to technological advancement.

Technology that increases productivity affects different sectors to varying degrees. Decreasing the need for labor drives inflation because fewer people are employed or need goods and services. However, the same technology also allows companies to produce more with fewer resources, resulting in deflation unless it is countered by increasing price levels so that revenue remains constant when less physical currency is available. The digital economy is where cryptocurrency becomes interesting as it provides variables other than the price/supply ratio to deflate the money supply relatively soundly and transparently.

Cryptocurrencies use complex algorithms and cryptography to produce new units of the currency with each block found on the network; they are created over time at an exponentially decreasing rate when all 21 million fixed units have been mined, that's it. No more digital tokens will ever exist after this point (this is what we call "deflation").

By nature, cryptocurrencies such as Bitcoin cannot be inflated by governments or banks secretly creating money out of thin air, nor can they be hacked or counterfeited due to their decentralized, secure P2P networks used worldwide by nodes that contain every user record for verification purposes via cryptography. This provides a significant degree of certainty that once you possess a unit of cryptocurrency, that ownership is recorded in the ledger and cannot be duplicated or stolen.

Although some other cryptocurrencies have different supply models, the ones with deflationary properties are more resistant to inflation by definition. This characteristic may seem counterintuitive for a currency but imagine how much risk you would take if your entire wealth were stored in printed pieces of paper! There is no real haven at this point, as even gold has lost 30% of its value since 2011 due to increased production.

The same logic applies to cryptocurrencies tied to the digital economy ecosystem; the money supply must grow each year; otherwise, their purchasing power goes down due to increased scarcity without new tokens entering circulation (there is fewer available token vs. existing total token supply). For 1 BTC to remain consistently worth $500 (which has indeed fluctuated in the past), you would need more people buying yearly. Additionally, because your investment does not generate any type of interest or dividend, you are stuck with 1 BTC all year long. Naturally, its demand should rise compared to fiat currencies with a low inflation rate.

WHAT MAKES BITCOIN SO DIFFERENT?

Bitcoin is not tied to any physical asset, so its price is determined solely by the number of people willing to acquire it. Unlike gold, no raw materials are involved in making a Bitcoin, so production cannot be ramped up when demand increases. The number of Bitcoins mined each time a block is solved has changed several times in the blockchain's lifetime, but overall it has been trending downwards per cycle. It halves every 4 years, and this mechanic alone acts as a solid deflationary force pushing all BTCs upwards in value over time.

This leads to the next question: What will make more people want to own digital tokens when they cannot be spent on anything other than paying transaction fees? If you haven't noticed yet, supply does not meet demand in cryptocurrency (many multi-millionaire investors are holding digital assets while merchant adoption is still low), mainly due to a lack of understanding or access to new markets.

The same type of restrictions that apply to fiat currencies also apply to cryptocurrencies; you cannot simply change it into cash or buy goods with it instantly. The process for doing so varies from one currency to another, but the technology is moving towards being able to spend your tokens easier, faster, and cheaper than before. If merchants could accept bitcoins directly without converting them into dollars/euros/yen, there would probably be more spending because their customers have explicitly asked them to!

CHAPTER 17

BASIC TERMINOLOGIES IN THE CRYPTOCURRENCY WORLD

There are many terms used in the cryptocurrency world that can be confusing for those who are new to the space. This section will define some of the most important terms you need to know.

Address: An address is a code to send, receive and store cryptocurrency.

Block: A record in the blockchain that contains several transactions.

Bitcoin: The first decentralized digital currency created by Satoshi Nakamoto

Blockchain: A public ledger that records all bitcoin transactions.

Cold storage wallet: It refers to keeping your crypto offline to avoid hacking and theft.

Cryptocurrency: A digital currency that uses cryptography to secure transactions and control the supply of units in circulation through mining, making it decentralized so no government or financial institutions can interfere with how much should be circulated.

Decentralized cryptocurrency: It is a digital currency with no central authority like the government to print money or make decisions.

Faucet: It is like a reward system that gives out free cryptocurrency (usually small amounts) to its users for completing captchas, watching ad videos, etc.

FOMO: stands for Fear of missing out and refers to a situation where an investor buys currencies like Bitcoin because they feel they might be getting too late to the party.

FUD: It stands for Fear Uncertainty and Doubt, used by cryptocurrency traders looking to sell their cryptocurrencies.

HODL: It is a misspelled intentional word that means to hold on for dear life when trading cryptocurrency in hopes of selling on an upswing.

ICO: Initial Coin Offering, a process used by new cryptocurrency firms looking to raise funds by offering digital tokens in exchange for cryptocurrencies like Bitcoin or Ether.

Genesis block: The first block in the blockchain of every cryptocurrency was created by Satoshi Nakamoto in January 2009.

Hashing: Cryptographic hashing is a technique used in creating digital fingerprints of the data. It's different for every file, so if you change one byte or character of that piece of information, it will completely change its fingerprint, making it unrecognizable to you and others using this service. This makes sure no one can tamper with the data.

Hot wallet: A cryptocurrency wallet that is connected to the internet. These are riskier because if you store your coins here, they can easily be hacked or stolen by anyone who knows how it works. It's best to use this for small amounts of money and transfer them into cold storage when not in need.

Mining: It is the process of verifying transactions and creating new blocks in a blockchain network. Miners use mining software/hardware to solve complex mathematical problems for each block created. If they succeed, new coins are rewarded per the cryptocurrency protocol's defined rules, ranging from 25-50 newly created coins.

Node: A device connected to a blockchain network that verifies and relays transactions from one user to another. Anyone can become a node on any cryptocurrency's network if they follow the rules of consensus protocol.

Private key: refers to a secret number or code known only by its owner for making cryptocurrency transactions.

Proof of work (POW) protocol: A system used by cryptocurrencies such as Bitcoin to validate and confirm the legitimacy of a transaction or data, making it tamper-proof and immutable. It requires miners or nodes in a blockchain network to compete against each other to solve complex mathematical problems using their computing power which gets more challenging with time and decreases the probability of solving it.

Proof Of Stake (POS) protocol: A consensus mechanism requires nodes to show ownership of specific amounts of cryptocurrency to verify transactions and earn rewards/newly created coins. This system doesn't require as much computing power as POW, thus making it eco-friendly but less secure.

Public key: A code that any sender can use to encrypt a message for its recipient. This is like your email address; you give it to everyone so they know how and where to send you emails. Still, the only difference here is that nobody knows what's inside or who sent them until they open it, making this a very secure way of communication.

Recipient: The person receiving cryptocurrency transactions, either an individual or a business entity.

Satoshi Nakamoto: An anonymous name/group who invented Bitcoin under this pseudonym in 2009 and disappeared without revealing their true identity even after media outlets made numerous attempts and journalists worldwide tried hard to find him/her/them!

Wallet: It is a piece of software or hardware used to store your cryptocurrency. You can install it on your computer or phone or use riskier web-based wallets because they're accessible from anywhere in the world and not secured behind walls like an app.

Whitelist: Refers to a list of accepted cryptocurrencies for crypto trading pairs that an exchange will support. This means you won't be able to buy/sell anything other than these coins with their help, so choose wisely before creating any transaction!

NFTS

CHAPTER 18

WHAT ARE NON-FUNGIBLE TOKENS (NFTS)?

NFTs are a new kind of cryptographic token representing ownership over digital or physical assets. The defining feature of NFTs is that each can be individually owned and differentiated from other tokens. The Ethereum community first proposed them as part of ERC-20, but they have since been implemented in many different blockchains, including EOS, Steem, and Tron. NFTs can represent assets such as identity claims (ERC-725), collectibles (ERC-1155), or other tokens from an existing platform like Ether. Your digital ownership over non-fungible items is called a "non-fungible token," hence the name!

It's important to remember that a blockchain is only required to transfer and store NFTs. You can own an asset without it being on a blockchain, but you need a decentralized public ledger to store your claims securely.

Non-fungible tokens (NFTs) are distinct from more prominent cryptocurrencies like Bitcoin - and the name gives it away.

A fungible item can be readily substituted with something identical. The $20 note is an excellent illustration of this - if I lend you a $20 bill, you won't notice if I return you a different $20 bill.

Non-fungible assets are the polar opposite. Consider a No. 1 Trainer Pokemon card, one of the rarest in the game's history, with just seven thoughts to be in existence. It may appear to be a regular card from a distance, but it has distinct features that distinguish it from others. If you lent THAT to a friend and received another back, you'd be furious.

Non-fungible tokens (NFTs) elevate the value of a commodity by adding this desirability and scarcity to the blockchain. They make it possible to build digitized versions of collectibles.

The first NFTs were CryptoKitties, allowing users to breed digital cats. Someone spent 600 ETH for a unique kitty in December 2017, worth around $1 million.

Non-fungible tokens, on the other hand, are exciting artists and gamers worldwide. Fans believe that non-fungible tokens will revolutionize art and gaming – providing tangible benefits to both industries. We've seen a recent spike in digital artwork; some masterpieces were sold at prestigious auction houses for hundreds of thousands of dollars. (Beeple, a well-known artist, created a piece called Ancient Technology depicting a retro Game Boy being built; it demonstrates how our technology has developed in just a few short years.)

For gamers, NFTs may revolutionize the gaming experience. They might be the precursor for rare in-game items traveling across titles. These assets could also be bought and sold on secondary marketplaces, potentially for cash, to create a sense of ownership among gamers. This will give players a feeling of possession over in-game extras presently available through games but seldom given.

COMPONENTS OF NFTS

The three major components of NFTs are:

- Nonunique tokens (not unique)

- Fungible tokens (interchangeable with others on the network)
- Unique assets (unique or one of a kind)

This type of digital property is completely different than what we understand digital to mean. We think of it as nonphysical, not true ownership, and a person can't control it. Crypto art has helped change that perception by offering something tangible as non-fungible tokens. It can also exist outside the self-contained world inside your computer desktop. Moreover, you can get creative and make your own NFTs to sell, or give away.

WHAT IS FUNGIBILITY?

Fungibility is the property of a good or asset whose individual units are capable of mutual substitution. It means that each item is essentially identical to every other. There are no specific traits that make one unique from another.

Fungibility is the quality of a commodity that states that each unit should replace any other. For example, you have two gold bars, one melted by mistake, making it somewhat distinct from the second. They should be identical since they are still 100 percent pure 24k gold. However, there will always be a difference between them, even when perfect circles aren't perfect, squares aren't square, or cubes aren't cube - and even when the corners of objects like that are perfectly straight. That means that if someone were to buy either bar, he would likely pay less for the "imperfect" looking object simply because its properties don't match his expectations based on previous experience with goods like these (there may also be legal issues involved as the "damaged" gold bar would likely have been stolen).

The fungibility of cryptocurrencies is very important for their adoption and widespread use. We can't expect people to embrace new technology if they don't feel safe using it because there's always a risk that someone else will try to steal your funds or counterfeit money. That means that we need some protection against such threats and one way this could be achieved is by making all tokens equally valuable, so nobody feels like he needs to spend his coins ASAP before another person takes them from him, etc. This also protects token owners from sudden price changes: imagine how you would feel about holding 100oz (~31kg) worth of gold today, valued at 100 USD/oz, but tomorrow it drops to 80 or even 20-30. You would likely sell some of your "gold" immediately, which means that the price will further drop until someone is willing to take over this bag of gold at a low cost because they believe in its future value. That's why fungibility is so crucial for cryptocurrencies - their values are constantly changing, and tokens need to be equally valuable if we don't want them to suffer from sudden losses all the time due to market fluctuations, etc.

WHAT ARE FUNGIBLE TOKENS?

Fungible tokens are the opposite of non-fungible tokens. Fungible means that another identical item or commodity can replace something without impacting other items. In other words, fungibility is an intrinsic property of a good or asset in which one unit is entirely interchangeable with another (e.g., one dollar equals two quarters), and no unique value is assigned to specific units.

Fungible tokens are often used in cryptocurrency and blockchain-based platforms to represent digital assets, such as currency, commodities, or loyalty points. They can be easily exchanged for other fungible tokens of the same type on a one-to-one basis. For example, Bitcoin (BTC) is a fungible token since each BTC can be exchanged for another BTC without affecting the value or utility of either token.

In contrast, non-fungible tokens are not interchangeable because each token represents a unique asset with its individualized characteristics. This uniqueness could be in the form of physical properties (e.g., diamonds), digital properties (e.g., MP three files), or even intangibles like voting rights or ownership stake in a company. Because of this, non-fungible tokens can often be considered "crypto collectibles" since another identical item cannot replace them.

One example of a fungible token is Bitcoin (BTC). As mentioned earlier, BTC is a digital asset that can be exchanged for another BTC on a one-to-one basis without affecting the value or utility of either token. In other words, each BTC is completely interchangeable with any other BTC - they are all worth the same amount and serve the same purpose.

Another example of a fungible token is Ethereum's Ether (ETH). ETH is also a digital asset that can be exchanged for another ETH on a one-to-one basis. However, unlike BTC, ETH is not used as a currency but as a "fuel" that powers the Ethereum network. This is because ETH is needed to pay transaction fees and execute smart contracts on the Ethereum blockchain.

As you can see, fungible tokens can take many forms depending on their intended use case. However, they all share one common trait - they are interchangeable with other identical tokens without affecting the value or utility of either token.

HOW NFT TOKENS WORK

One of the most important aspects of understanding NFTs is that each one has a specific value assigned by its creator. This can be configured anytime, depending on what the user wants their token to represent or achieve.

NFTs are a new kind of cryptographic token representing ownership over digital or physical assets. The defining feature of NFTs is that each can be individually owned and differentiated from other tokens. The Ethereum community first proposed them as part of ERC-20, but they have since been implemented in many different blockchains, including EOS, Steem, and Tron.

NFTs can represent assets such as identity claims (ERC-725), collectibles (ERC-1155), or other tokens from an existing platform like Ether. For example, CryptoKitties utilizes non-fungible kitty "tokens" on their blockchain to represent unique cats with distinct features; when a cat is bred with a different cat, the offspring will have distinct features shared from its parents.

To date, the most popular use case for NFTs is as collectibles. In this context, users buy and trade unique digital goods on a blockchain to secure ownership of those items without any centralized entity controlling them. This gives buyers confidence in knowing their item won't be duplicated or faked since each token has its own identity assigned from its creator with an immutable record stored on a blockchain.

NFT tokens can also represent non-fungible entities such as tickets (ERC-901) or certificates (ERC-725). However, it's important to note that even though these assets may vary slightly, they're still categorized as fungible because one asset represents exactly another unit of the same asset.

WHY DO WE CARE ABOUT OWNING DIGITAL ASSETS?

Everything exists as data in today's world, where information lives everywhere -- from email messages to PDF documents, social media posts, and more. We have access to countless datasets that describe our daily lives: things like online banking statements or medical records that belong to us because they contain personal information such as health histories or financial transactions. But there's one major problem with this data-driven society: much of it is still ephemeral since it's held by third parties who control it. Unless you encrypt your data and store the keys yourself, others will always be able to access that information simply because they can prove that they have it (i.e., "you sent me this email"). This is where blockchains come into play: on a blockchain, data ownership is managed through cryptographic tokens, which allow us to securely transfer claims between one another while preventing unauthorized changes or deletions of any content. We'll explore these concepts more later on!

CHAPTER 19

HISTORY OF NFTS

Generation NFTs were created during the Ethereum blockchain's early days in 2015. The very first NFT was CryptoPets, which was a digital collectible game. Players could purchase, breed, and sell virtual pets in the game.

Since then, the use of NFTs has exploded. Now, there are all sorts of different applications for NFTs. For example, they can be used to represent real-world assets like property or artwork. Or they can be used to create digital experiences like video games or virtual worlds.

The possibilities are endless! And that's why I believe that Blockchain technology and NFTs will shape the future of business and entertainment as we know it.

2012-2016 - THE EARLY HISTORY OF NFTS

Long before Ethereum existed, the concept that became the driving force of NFTs was already thought up. In 2012, a paper by Meni Rosenfield introduced the 'Colored Coins' concept for the Bitcoin blockchain.

The idea of Colored Coins was to describe a class of methods for representing and managing real-world assets on the blockchain to prove ownership of those assets, similar to regular Bitcoins, but with an added 'token' element that determines their use, making them segregated and unique.

The limitations of Bitcoin meant that the Colored Coins concept could never be realized; however, it did lay the foundation for the experiments that led to the invention of NFTs.

On May 3rd, 2014, digital artist Kevin McCoy minted the first-known NFT 'Quantum' on the Namecoin blockchain. 'Quantum' is a digital image of a pixelated octagon that hypnotically changes color and pulsates in a manner reminiscent of an octopus.

After these events, significant experimentation and development occurred, and platforms were built on the Bitcoin blockchain. The Ethereum blockchain also started its initial reign over NFTs.

The Counterparty platform (Bitcoin 2.0) was established and gained ground as a platform enabling digital assets creation.

Spells of Genesis followed close behind in the footsteps of Counterparty and began pioneering in the issuing of in-game assets.

2016 beckoned on the age of the meme and saw the release of a host of Rare Pepes NFTs on the Counterparty platform.

Important to note, however, is that the Bitcoin blockchain was never intended to be used as a database for tokens representing the ownership of assets, and thus began the significant shift for NFTs to the Ethereum blockchain.

2017-2020 - NFTS GO MAINSTREAM

The significant shift for NFTs to Ethereum was backed up by introducing a set of token standards, allowing the creation of tokens by developers. The token standard is a subsidiary of the smart contract standard, including informing developers how to create, issue and deploy new tokens in line with the underlying blockchain technology.

Two software developers, John Watkinson and Matt Hall followed up the success of the Rare Pepes with their generative series of NFTs on the Ethereum blockchain, which they branded as CryptoPunks. CryptoPunks are considered some of the first NFTs created and originally offered for free. The experimental project, limited to 10,000 pieces with no two characters the same, was inspired by London punk culture and the cyberpunk movement.

During the world's largest hackathon for the Ethereum ecosystem, the Vancouver-based venture studio Axiom Zen introduced CryptoKitties.

CryptoKitties is a virtual game based on the Ethereum blockchain; the game enables players to adopt, breed, and trade virtual cats, storing them in crypto wallets. After its announcement, it wasn't long before the game became a viral sensation, becoming so popular that CryptoKitties clogged the Ethereum blockchain, and people began making unbelievable profits.

Following the huge success of CryptoKitties, NFT gaming began to gain momentum and move forward, with NFTS gathering increasingly more public attention.

NFT gaming and metaverse projects were in the spotlight, and the first to break ground in this space was Decentraland (MANA), a decentralized VR platform on the Ethereum blockchain. Decentraland is an open-world gaming platform that allows players to explore, play games, build, collect items, and more, and everything that you find, earn and build there, you own on the blockchain.

It wasn't long before other platforms and games using Enjin Coin (ENJ) appeared on the scene, allowing developers to tokenize their in-game items on Ethereum, giving those in-game items a value in the real world.

Another blockchain-based trade and battle game also emerged, Axie Infinity (AXS), a game that is partially owned and operated by its players.

2021 - THE YEAR OF THE NFT

2021 became the year of the NFT and a huge explosion and surge in NFT supply and demand.

One of the most significant factors in this boom was the huge changes that occurred within the art market and the industry at large when prestigious auction houses, Christie's and Sotheby's, not only took their auctions into the online world but also began selling NFT art.

This led to Christie's record-breaking sale of Beeple's Everyday: the First 5000 Days NFT for $69 million. Such a huge sale from such a prestigious auction house validated the NFT marketplace significantly.

As well as the surge in demand for NFTs that resulted from the famous Christie's auction, another knock-on effect was other blockchains getting involved and starting their versions of NFTs. These included blockchains such as Cardano, Solano, Tezos, and Flow. With these newer platforms for NFTs, some new standards were established to ensure the authenticity and uniqueness of the digital assets created.

Towards the end of the year, once Facebook rebranded as Meta and moved into the metaverse, the surge in NFT demand, especially within the metaverse, was remarkable.

CHAPTER 20

ADVANTAGES OF NFTS

The NFTs have several advantages over the fungible tokens. They provide more granular ownership since each token is unique and can be tracked through a public ledger. If an asset has been divided into multiple shares, each share will correspond to its unique token on Ethereum's blockchain.

Non-fungible tokens provide a new layer to digital interactions. NFTs offer several advantages over conventional currencies. The three most essential benefits of NFTs are:

Ownership and provenance: A single NFT can represent a unique real-world object, such as an original work of art. The token's ownership history is recorded on the blockchain, which cannot be replicated or forged. This creates a clear audit trail and provenance for the token.

Rare: The scarcity of NFTs is what gives them value. Although non-fungible token creators are free to make as many tokens as they want, they frequently restrict the amount produced to enhance rarity and value.

Digital: each item exists in digital form (crypto-assets like CryptoKitties or ERC-20 tokens are the most common NFTs, but this definition could also apply to things like movie tickets and event badges).

Indivisible: Although the precise formation of non-fungible tokens is not set in stone, they are generally divided into smaller parts. You must either buy the entire value of digital artwork or nothing at all.

Digital scarcity: With fungible tokens, one unit is like another (e.g., two $20 notes). But with NFTs, each token has its distinct value based on characteristics such as age, rarity, condition, etc. This allows for new forms of digital scarcity with corresponding economic advantages over traditional currencies;

They're transferable: NFTs can be transferred from one owner to another.

Uniqueness: They are unique, which means that once a token is bought or created, it cannot be replicated in the same way as traditional tokens. For example, if someone creates a rare art piece and sells ten prints of this work, nothing prevents these copies from being freely traded on online markets. At the same time, each original artwork has an immutable history recorded on the blockchain. This ensures authenticity and provenance for any NFT asset using cryptographic proofs instead of relying on third parties such as centralized institutions or marketplaces like eBay. The advantage here is greater transparency since all transactions between buyers and sellers will be recorded publicly, and information about previous ownerships.

Interoperability across games and ecosystems: Non-Fungible Tokens provide interoperability between multiple platforms and projects, creating a whole ecosystem where consumers can seamlessly move from one platform to another without losing their progress.

CHAPTER 21

NON-FUNGIBLE TOKEN USE CASES

NFTs have a wide variety of potential use cases. Some of the most popular include:

GAMING

NFTs are gaining traction in gaming since they address some of the industry's inherent challenges. For instance, top games such as Fortnite prohibit the sale of uncommon features and add-ons such as weapons and skins.

With NFTs, however, these characteristics can readily be moved and utilized in other games. As a result, non-fungible tokens may assist in establishing game economies.

DIGITAL ASSETS

Non-Fungible tokens are a way to stand out from the crowd. They allow you to be unique, even in this time of digitalization and conformity.

However, there is more than just being different for its sake. In some cases, it might make good sense to have an NFT that corresponds with your real-world identity or something else about you as a person - such as artwork created by yourself! Imagine if every artwork had a tokenized version on Ethereum. People would own their masterpieces while not having them locked away in galleries or relying on centralized platforms like Medium or Instagram, which can change policies at any moment without prior notice leaving artists unable to upload new content.

IDENTITY

An NFT is a perfect vehicle for establishing your identity on Ethereum. It can be used to prove you are whom you say you are, empowering people with their data and giving them back control over it. A person's ID token could store information such as name, birthday, or eye color, which would make identifying that individual possible in case of loss or theft - but also when they need access to some service without having a centralized institution do the authentication for them (e.g., blockchain-based job portals).

Tokenized Artwork Blockchain technology has seen its fair share of critics over the years, especially after Bitcoin was involved in illegal activities like the Silk Road marketplace, where drugs were sold using BTCs. However, history always repeats itself - people first use it to do bad things when something new is created. It should not be the case with blockchain technology, though - it has many great potentials, like tokenizing assets (e.g., art), which can then be traded or even sold on online auction sites without having a third-party entity involved.

NFTs validate identity in various ways, including proof of identification for non-fungible game tickets.

COLLECTIBLES

Non-fungible tokens are the perfect medium for collectibles since they allow people to get something unique, unlike an identical twin. Imagine if you could have your very own fidget spinner that couldn't be copied or forged. Things like this can gain much value over time, and NFTs put them on the blockchain, making them immutable - no one can change their properties later on! There has been some debate about whether non-fungible items should be considered digital assets rather than collectibles. Still, in reality, it's really up to each person to use these new types of tokens. Just imagine owning things from history, such as moon rocks or even baguette coins from France during Napoleonic times - that would be cool!

These are just a few of the many ways that NFTs can be used. It's still early days for this technology, and we are only beginning to scratch the surface of its potential. So far, NFTs have mainly been used for gaming, digital assets, identity, and collectibles - but who knows what else will be possible in the future? Stay tuned to find out!

CHAPTER 22

HOW TO START USING NFTS

OpenSea and Rarible are the leading platforms for NFT creation. While Rarible dominates total sales figures, OpenSea provides more related services, including the ability to create your own NFT webstore powered by the OpenSea exchange. Both platforms allow users to upload their art and create collections without technical blockchain knowledge.

Before you get started, know there will be some upfront costs. NFTs are powered by a blockchain - typically Ethereum's blockchain. Using a blockchain comes at a cost, a network fee called gas that you'll likely need to pay to tokenize your art.

Rarible requires artists to mint their NFTs on the blockchain (on-chain) during creation. This means repeated smaller costs. If you're planning on selling a couple of NFTs for huge prices, Rarible is likely your best bet. On the other hand, if you want to create a multitude of cheaper NFTs, you'll want to use OpenSea's Collection Manager.

OpenSea Collection Manager allows users to pay a one-time fee for establishing a new collection. From that collection, an unlimited number of NFTs can be created and stored off-chain by the OpenSea centralized team until a sale is made. At this point, the buyer will pay the gas fee associated with the transaction, and your NFT will be placed on the chain and transferred.

SET UP METAMASK.

The first thing you'll need to do to make your own NFT is to set up a software wallet. This wallet can hold your NFTs, and you'll also need to use it to pay blockchain gas fees later.

Make your way over to metamask.io, where you can download the app or add the chrome extension. Creating a MetaMask wallet is simple and free. Remember to keep track of your seed phrase if you need to recover the wallet. You can also download the MetaMask app on Android or iOS, but it is a bit clunkier than the browser extension.

Remember that wallets don't hold cryptocurrency or NFTs — they store your private key, which is needed to authorize transactions. All cryptocurrencies and NFTs are kept on the blockchain with the wallet ID designating ownership.

TOKENIZE YOUR ART OR OTHER ASSETS.

Once you have a MetaMask wallet created, you'll be able to create your own NFTs.

Navigate to opensea.io and click the Create button in the menu bar. Now you can connect your MetaMask wallet with OpenSea and get to work.

Create a name for your NFT collection, then click the Add New Item button. You are now ready to upload the file you want to tokenize and give it certain properties and stats to distinguish it from the rest of your collection. Determine how many copies you want of each item, then set a retail price

LIST ON THE MARKETPLACE.

To sell your first NFT, you'll need to enable OpenSea to sell items from your account. This requires a blockchain transaction, so you'll have to pay a gas fee. Send some Ether to your MetaMask, and you're good to go. You'll only need to pay this fee the first time you create an NFT collection.

If you don't have any Ethereum, you can use eToro to purchase some and send it to your MetaMask wallet. If you're completely new to cryptocurrencies, it may be helpful to start with Benzinga's guide to buying Ethereum.

CHAPTER 23

PICKING THE PERFECT NFT MARKETPLACE FOR YOU

For example, if I want to buy CryptoKitties that are also limited edition, then CryptoKittyDex is the perfect place for me. If I'm looking for novelty items or unique NFTs, RareBits should be my pick.

The same should go for you. It all depends on your expectations and preferences. Do you want to buy a simple one of the multi-NFT collections? Then find an ordinary exchange with reasonable prices for buying or selling. Are you patient enough to invest in NFT markets and search for rarities and crypto collectibles? Go ahead and use decentralized apps (Dapps).

TOP NFT MARKETPLACES

Here are some of the most popular NFT marketplaces right now.

1. OPENSEA

OpenSea is the most successful NFT platform. OpenSea provides a wide range of digital assets on its platform, and it's free to join and look around. It also supports creators and individuals and has an easy-to-use procedure for creating your own NFT (also known as "minting").

OpenSea, a decentralized marketplace for NFTs, is named appropriately. The platform's name is appropriate since it supports approximately 150 distinct payment tokens. OpenSea is an excellent introduction to the NFT world.

2. AXIE MARKETPLACE

The online shop for the video games Axie Infinity is called Axie Marketplace. Axies are mythical creatures that may be bought and trained and then pitted against other players' Axies to earn rewards. Players on Axie Marketplace can purchase new characters, entire islands, and other goods as NFTs for use in the game.

The Ethereum blockchain is the foundation for Axie Infinity tokens (also known as Axie Shards). As a result, they may be bought and sold on various other NFT marketplaces, as well as some cryptocurrency exchanges such as Coinbase Global (NASDAQ: COIN).

3. LARVA LABS/CRYPTOPUNKS

The most well-known Larva Laboratories product is the viral CryptoPunks NFT project. They were initially offered for free in 2017, but some CryptoPunks have sold for millions of dollars since then. Other digital art efforts by Larva Labs include Autoglyphs and other Ethereum blockchain-based software development projects.

The CryptoPunks NFTs from Larva Labs are sold out but maybe bid on and purchased from third-party marketplaces. Nonetheless, keep an eye on Larva Labs' numerous projects, including the Meebits, which can be purchased directly through the company's built-in marketplace.

4. NBA TOP SHOT MARKETPLACE

The NBA and the WNBA's first NFT project is NBA Top Shot. Collectible moments (video clips and play highlights) and art from the world's top basketball leagues may be acquired on its market.

The NBA developed it as a closed market (you can only buy and sell on Top Shot) with Dapper Labs' Flow blockchain. It's simple to join up and purchase goods right on the marketplace website. Collectible moments may be purchased for as little as a few dollars each.

5. RARIBLE

Another large marketplace for all types of NFTs is Rarable. The platform allows you to buy, sell, or produce any type of art, film, collectibles, or music. However, unlike OpenSea, you'll have to utilize the marketplace's cryptocurrency Rarible (CRYPTO: RARI), to purchase and trade on the site. Rarible is based on the Ethereum blockchain (although artwork may be handled using OpenSea tokens as well).

Rarable has teamed up with some well-known businesses. Taco Bell, owned by Yum! Brands (NYSE: YUM) has employed Rarable to add the artwork to its site. Adobe recently collaborated with Rarable to help protect NFT artists' and creators' work, as Adbe (NASDAQ: ADBE) does.

6. SUPERRARE

SuperRare, like Rarable, is creating a marketplace for digital artists. The site includes pictures, films, and 3D models, but purchases can be made using Ethereum instead of money.

SuperRare just announced its cryptocurrency named SuperRare, which is based on the Ethereum network. The tokens will be used to discover and promote new talent on the market. Rarable NFTs, like OpenSea, can also be purchased and sold by SuperRare NFTs.

7. FOUNDATION

The Foundation. The app was created as a simple, no-frills platform for purchasing digital art. Ethereum is used to sell goods. More than $100 million worth of NFTs has been sold since the marketplace's inception in early 2021.

The Foundation community invites artists to the platform, and purchasers only need a funded Ethereum wallet to start purchasing. If you're searching for a quick and easy method to begin creating your own NFTs, Foundation isn't the best spot to start, but the marketplace does contain plenty of artwork in a straightforward style that you can peruse.

8. NIFTY GATEWAY

Nifty Gateway has helped to sell several of the most well-known digital artists, such as Beeple and singer/musician Grimes. It's an art curation platform powered by Gemini (owned by the Winklevoss twins), a cryptocurrency exchange. The NFTs, or Nifties, are based on Ethereum.

Nifty Gateway also offers LUTs for purchase, just like the Gemini platform. Although you don't keep NFTs in your wallet, they are maintained by Nifty Gateway and Gemini because they are curated platforms. While this may not be ideal for collectors who want greater control over their art investments, NFT purchases and sales can be made in fiat currency (e.g., USD) without making a crypto transaction first.

9. MINTABLE

Mintable, backed by Mark Cuban, wants to be an open market similar to OpenSea. To use Mintable, you'll need Ethereum. The platform also enables the creation of NFTs for artists of all types (from photographers to musicians) who want to sell their work as digital assets.

An aspiring NFT collector or maker must acquire Ethereum from a crypto exchange, then connect their wallet to Mintable to use the marketplace.

10. THETA DROP

Theta is a blockchain platform that aims to offer decentralized video and TV distribution on the internet. The NFT marketplace Theta Drop debuted in 2021 with the World Poker Tour's digital collectibles. The World Poker Tour was an early adopter of ThetaTV, using it to broadcast material online.

Theta uses the Theta Blockchain. You'll need THETA tokens to participate in the Theta Drop NFT marketplace (CRYPTO: THETA). Various crypto exchanges, including Binance, support THETA, and the assets purchased with them may be stored in a cryptocurrency wallet and Theta's crypto wallet app.

CHAPTER 24

HOW TO MAKE AND SELL AN NFTS

A step-by-step tutorial on creating and selling an NFT if you want to give it a go with your digital work.

Many artists are asking how to construct and market an NFT these days. Non-fungible tokens continue to stir debate and elicit outrage due to the eye-watering prices that some pieces of NFT art have sold for. It's only natural that you'd be curious if NFTs provide a possibility to profit from your creative work if that's the case. This book will assist you in understanding how to make and sell an NFT if that is the case.

However, these are exceptional cases, and even if you replicate their success, you'll generally discover that the bulk of the money won't flow to you. The firms that facilitate transactions and the platforms that generate and maintain NFTs charge fees to NFT artists up-front and after any sale, and they may even leave you out of pocket based on the price your work sells for.

There are several online platforms where you can create and sell NFTs right now. OpenSea, Rarible, SuperRare, Nifty Gateway, Foundation, VIV3, BakerySwap, Axie Marketplace, and NFT ShowRooom are popular auction sites for buying and selling NFTs. Payment options include MetaMask, Torus, Portis, WalletConnec, Coinbase, MyEtherWallet, and Fortmatic.

Buy some cryptocurrency Ethereum cryptocurrency; most platforms accept ether.

First, you'll have to pay a platform to "mint" (or generate) your piece. Most platforms want to cover the cost with ether, the cryptocurrency native to the open-source blockchain platform Ethereum, where NFTs first debuted.

Keep in mind that, like bitcoin and many other cryptocurrencies, the value of ether (abbreviated as ETH) is prone to huge fluctuations. From under $1,000 in 2021 to over $4,800 in 2021, with numerous peaks and valleys on the road, it's been known to swing by hundreds of dollars in hours.

To acquire Ethereum, you'll need to construct a "digital wallet" and link it to your NFT platform of choice. Several digital wallet services are available, but we'll use MetaMask, which is available as a browser plugin and a mobile app for this purpose. If you'd instead utilize another provider or are familiar with digital wallets and have your own already, go straight to step 4.

CREATE A DIGITAL WALLET

To create a MetaMask digital wallet, go to the website and click on the blue 'Download' button in the top-right corner. We selected to install the browser extension because we're using a desktop computer, but there is also a mobile app.

When you first launch your wallet, it will prompt you to 'generate a new wallet and seed phrase.' You shouldn't be concerned about what "seed phrase" means (it's simply a list of words that saves blockchain data). Say yes, then it's merely a case of agreeing to the conditions, creating a password, and going through some security checks to get your account up and running.

ADD MONEY TO YOUR WALLET.

You'll need to add some ETH to your MetaMask wallet or any other digital wallet after you've created it. That's not difficult: simply click the 'Buy' button and pick Wyre as your payment method. You'll be taken to a screen where you can buy ETH with Apple Pay or a debit card. If you'd rather not spend money, feel free to proceed; all you have to do is wait a little longer.

CONNECT YOUR WALLET TO AN NFT PLATFORM

The general workflow of setting up a digital wallet is similar across all platforms. Once you've got some ETH in your digital wallet available to spend, you may go to the NFT platform of your choice and start creating your NFT. We're using Rarable as an example for this purpose, but there are numerous other NFT platforms to explore.

Rarable is one of several digital collectible marketplaces.

To access Rarable, go to Rarable.com. In the right-hand corner of the screen, there's a button that says 'Connect wallet.' Click here to connect your wallet with MetaMask. A popup will appear asking whether you want to link your wallet with Rarable. Select "Yes," then "Connect," and agree to the terms of service before confirming your age.

UPLOAD YOUR FILE

GIFs can be used as NFTs; however, we recommend you create the file in an image editor like Photoshop or Paint .NET because they give full control over sizing and sharpness. To do this: Open your chosen software and create a new image of dimension 256 x 128 using black and white colors (if using Paint.NET, make sure Advanced Mode is on). Paste your GIF into that new image, and scale it to fit the full image.

You're ready to make your NFT now. The blue 'Create' button in the upper right should be clicked. After that, you may select a single one-off project or sell the same item several times. Choose 'Single' in this example. You must upload the digital file you wish to convert into an NFT at this stage. Rarible accepts PNG, GIF, WEBP, MP4, and MP3 files up to 30MB.

Upload your file; you'll see a preview of your NFT post on the right.

SET UP AN AUCTION

Choose the settings for your auction

In the next part of the form, you'll need to choose how you want to sell your NFT artwork. There are three options here. 'Fixed price' allows you to set a price and sell to someone instantly (like 'Buy it now on eBay'). 'Unlimited Auction' will enable people to carry on making bids until you accept one. Finally, a 'Timed auction' is an auction that only takes place for a specific time. That's the option we'll choose for our example.

The hard part now begins: establishing a minimum price. Set it too low, and you'll lose money on each sale because of the high costs. We'll set our price at 1 ETH and allow people seven days to make offers.

You'll be able to purchase it immediately, but before you do, there's an option to "Unlock once purchased." This allows you to give your future buyer a complete, high-resolution copy of your work and other material via a hidden website or download link. The option labeled 'Choose Collection' is the most perplexing. This is a somewhat technical question regarding how the blockchain works. The default option is "Rarible," so we recommend you leave it that way.

DESCRIBE YOUR NFT

You may now add a title and description to your item's listing. To increase the chances of selling your NFT, take some time to consider this. You'll be shown a questionnaire that asks you to choose what proportion of royalties you want to earn from any future resale of your work.

There's a further balancing act this time: higher percentages will earn you more money over time, but they'll also deter people from reselling your work since they'll be less likely to profit for themselves. Finally, the file properties may be added as an optional field. You're almost done at this point.

PAY THE FEE

Click 'Create Item' to begin the listing procedure. You'll be prompted to connect your wallet if you don't have enough money. If you don't have enough money in your wallet, don't worry; you won't have to start over. Click on the wallet symbol in the top-right corner of the screen to add money directly within Rarable.

Just a word of caution before you do so. The listing fee may appear relatively low, as in our case: $5.91. However, this is only the beginning of the costs you'll be subjected to. To generate your NFT, you must first agree to a further charge of $42.99 before proceeding further in our situation. Aside from the fees for buying and selling NFTs, there will also be a commission payment when someone buys your asset and a transfer cost to execute the transaction. From our perspective, none of this was adequately clarified on Rarable's website when we tried it.

CHAPTER 25

MUST-KNOW NFT PRINCIPLES AND TERMINOLOGY

Are you new to the NFT industry? Don't worry; you're not the only one. However, you'll undoubtedly encounter words that are new to you. Some are specific to the NFT sector, while others come from other domains. Let's take a look at some and get you up to speed!

NFT: Non-Fungible Token or CryptoArtwork, a digital asset with unique properties.

ERC-20 Tokens: Ethereum smart contracts for tokens that implement the ERC token standard (see below). The most common NFTs are based on the ERC 20 token. These tokens conform to the commonly known and well-established principles around cryptocurrency, including fungibility and transparency, two important features we want in our art assets! There will be many more types of tokens coming up as time goes by but don't worry; you can still use them even if they're not like ETH/BTC/LTC, etc. The best part about this industry is its highly collaborative nature - everyone's open to sharing their research and findings, all in the name of advancing our industry.

ERC Token Standard: A set of rules that smart contracts on Ethereum have to implement, thus allowing them to easily interact with each other without requiring any central party or third party's involvement. The ERC token standard forms a base for fungible tokens (like ETH), which can be used as currency and allows non-fungible tokens to create artworks like CryptoPunks!

1/1: A "one of a kind" or "1/1" is a one-of-a-kind piece of art. A 1/1 may be a stand-alone NFT (e.g., as produced by a digital artist), or it may also be a super rare 1/1 incorporated into a more extensive generative set. (Technically, all items within such sets are technically unique, even if they aren't labeled.)

Ape: NFTs are a relatively new form of cryptocurrency, and the term "ape" is unique to their world. It refers to the Bored Ape Yacht Club, one of the blue-chip OG generative NFT sets (arguably the gold standard among NFT drops, with top-quality, whimsical generative art and insanely high values per NFT). The phrase has different meanings. As a verb - to ape or to enter - it may mean "to purchase," "to buy in early," or "to rise in value." However, it's flexible too. For example, one can say, "That's going to be an ape-level drop!"

CryptoPunk: CryptoPunks are non-fungible tokens (NFT) based on the ERC 20 token standard. These NFTs were initially produced as part of Matt Hall's '90s Neon Dystopia' project in 2017 - they're punk characters from this sci-fi universe! They all have different attributes like names, weights & heights so that you can tell them apart, just like real people or Pokemon cards! The original collection of CryptoPunks contains over 300 different characters, but new ones will be added all the time!

CryptoKitty: The original artwork for a Cryptokitty is created by combining several traits. There are many possible variations within each trait set, and these combinations create an almost limitless amount of unique artworks - this means no two kitties can ever truly be identical. They're like real cats in that way, too, except they can't breed…at least not yet anyway...

Diamondhands: This is the group of NFT investors in it for the long run. They're long-term investors who trust in the big payoff to come.

Drop: An NFT sale is known as a drop. It may be a noun, such as "that was an incredible release!" Or it can be a verb, such as "When will that item be available?"

Floor: The floor, often within a more extensive set, is the cheapest price an NFT (typically) purchases. NFT buyers are constantly on the lookout for floor bargains, and it's frequent to have special lanes in project Discords focused on analyzing the floor - why it's where it is, where it's going, what happened to it previously, etc.

FOMO: FOMO stands for Fear of Missing Out. It's a psychological phenomenon that occurs when someone feels they're going to miss out on something great if they don't buy it now - like CryptoPunks and other NFTs!

NFT: This is the acronym we use to mean non-fungible token, which means your piece of art can never be traded or sold again. There will only ever be one copy, so you know no one else could replicate what you have - it's yours forever!

Open Source Artworks & Community Projects: Open source artwork refers to projects whose codebase is open-sourced under public domain/CC0 licenses (typically), so anyone can access their design files, software, etc., learn from them, and create similar projects.

Punk: A Punk is a CryptoArt NFT that can be collected or traded on the blockchain. They're unique digital works of art with different traits which you can buy for your collection!

Resale Value: Anytime an NFT is sold at market rate (which will vary from sale to sale), its resale value is set as part of the equation. More expensive pieces tend to have higher resale values because they hold their value better over time - this makes sense since there's less demand for lower-priced items, even if they are incredibly rare or desirable within a project community! This means someone interested in reselling may pay more upfront to get a higher price item worth more later.

Sales: Sales are where NFTs can be purchased, and they're known as drops! Drops vary depending on their nature - some coins have monthly releases that happen at a specific time & date (like CryptoPunks). Others may offer tokens for free through community projects or contests, but no matter what, there's always something new coming out every month!

Tokenization: This is when artworks become non-fungible tokens (NFT) by being turned into blockchain assets with unique attributes using ERC 20 token standards. Each artwork becomes its one-of-a-kind piece! Tokens provide visual artists with an alternative way to distribute digital collectibles without worrying about setting up an online store. With non-fungible tokens, anyone can instantly create a new token and distribute it to any number of users in just two simple steps!

Tokenomics: The science behind the vision. Cryptoart's Tokenomics is not focused on creating more market value that would drive speculative investments but instead seeks out real demands, resulting in genuine sales with true collectors who support our artists. We've developed this model for crypto-economic stability. Hence, all NFTs hold their resale values over time & within each project community without volatility due to speculation or other factors outside artwork demand. This means there is no need to hoard as selling at a market rate also sets your floor price - you're always guaranteed a fair return!

FUD: This is the acronym for Fear, Uncertainty & Doubt. It's a strategy that some people use to scare investors into selling their tokens or coins by spreading false information about companies - like Crypto art!

GAS: This term is used for the fees you pay to execute smart contracts on the Ethereum network. It's based on how complex your contract code is and depends on other factors, so it might vary from transaction to transaction!

CryptoArt Gallery & CryptoCollectibles Showroom: These are physical galleries where fine art inspired by blockchain technology is displayed! Our first Crypto collectibles showroom was located at Blockchain Summit in Chicago this May - it featured work from our artist friends who have been involved with Cryptoart since its inception, as well as some brand new artists we're working with too. The second showroom will be based in San Francisco at our offices!

Tokenized Art Show: This is an event that Cryptoart co-organized with the Blockchain Investors Consortium (BIC) to highlight blockchain-inspired fine art. The show included many of Cryptoart's artists, including Cryptograffiti, whose work was shown for the first time publicly outside his community - you can read more about it here if interested :)

IPFS: This protocol distributes files throughout the web to ensure their permanence! It can take some time for specific content, like high-resolution images or videos, to be distributed, so there are websites where you can preview them if needed.

IPFS Hash: This is similar to an ID number that allows anyone with internet access who knows this hash string to find your work on IPFS - no need for complicated file-sharing links! There's more info about how it works here :)

MetaMask: A bridge that lets you visit the distributed web of tomorrow in your browser today. You can install MetaMask as a Chrome extension and then use it every day just like any other chrome plugin without ever needing our command-line tools or having to deal with complex wallets or tokens.

Tokenized Artwork Database: This project aims to create a comprehensive catalog of all artwork associated with non-fungibility on Ethereum. Hence, collectors have an easier time discovering new pieces & artists who want exposure without going through intermediaries. We'll bring together different media types, including images, audio, and video, to showcase our community's work in the best way possible!

Value of Artwork: The importance of artwork is subjective - it's whatever someone wants to pay for something at any given time. This means the market determines prices instead of some objective standard, which makes the art very special because there can't be a substitute or replacement for this type of creativity no matter how much technology advances :)

Wallet Address: A wallet address lets anyone send you tokens but only with your permission, so they must know your public key - that's why it's important to never share these strings with people who might try and take advantage :(Wallet addresses let us manage our crypto assets securely & privately without giving out personal info like email addresses, real names, etc. Some artists use them anonymously as well!

Metadata: You can add any type of metadata (the info that describes and explains things) you like to your artwork to make them more searchable online! If we want our work recognized by the community, we need people to be able to find it :) This is possible because decentralized apps like Cryptoart.com let us customize the data associated with each piece - anything from the artist's name & biography to the location where the artwork was created or even what kind of mood its creator was in when they made it ;)

Mint: This is when you print a physical artwork, and it's often done in limited edition, so only the number of copies specified is created. Crypto art does not provide this service, but artists can do it themselves if they want to!

Moon: This is just a cute way to say someone's work has gone viral :) It can also mean that something becomes popular quickly - this slang term was initially used in the cryptocurrency community, but it applies to other things too!

NFTy Mag: Nifty magazine aims at providing an artistic perspective on all things blockchain & decentralized, which means they write articles about art, music, and culture from time to time. They're currently looking for new writers, so if you want your voice heard by others or simply need some extra cash while building up your portfolio, feel free to apply here :D

Listed Artists: The following artists are already part of Cryptoart's collection with their page where fans can see more info, including their bio & the print edition size of their artwork.

LFT: This stands for letterform token and represents physical letters from artists to their fans. You can check out examples here if interested! These are non-fungible as well, so each has its unique code, which makes them collectible items :)

Makers: In cryptoart, makers refer to those who create & design artwork using digital currency like Ether or other ERC20 tokens associated with specific projects. It's all done online without any intermediaries because we believe creators should have control over what they do :) Makers often sell limited edition pieces through galleries, but many offer smaller batches directly to customers too!

Opensea: Opensea is a decentralized marketplace for art and collectibles that supports NFTs, so you can buy & sell authentic, verified digital creations there! It has its open-source token too, called OSC, which artists can create & distribute as they please :)

Proof Art: This form of art uses cryptographic proof of work to create each artwork by spending computer power to solve complex mathematical puzzles related to the CryptoNote protocol. The resulting non-fungible tokens (including prints) contain placements of certain data blocks from a Monero blockchain which make them one of a kind :) You can see an example here - a picture of two letters I sent to someone recently.

Engraving: This term refers to X-ray images of a Monero blockchain transaction so you can see all the data stored in a given token. It's all encrypted, of course, but Cryptoart takes extra precautions by watermarking images to protect the artist's work from being copied, sold, or altered without their consent!

Paperhands: This is the name of a Cryptoart project that lets authors generate paper wallets for NFTs they create. Read more about it here, then visit paper.cryptoart.com to see what's possible!

OpenSea: This is another decentralized marketplace where crypto collectors can buy & sell unique tokens :) It supports all ERC20 & ERC721 tokens, including artwork by Cryptoart :) You can get started there right now, either using their mobile app or browsing through listings on the website. If you like something, make sure you see if it's available in your favorite currency (that would be Ether) before asking sellers to accept other forms of payment :)

QRL: QRL stands for quantum-resistant ledger and refers to a type of network built based on advanced cryptography. Other ERC20 tokens can be created for this ledger, but it does not support NFTs yet, so Cryptoart is always looking to work with QRL developers to create non-fungible tokens there!

CryptoSlate: This is an online directory that provides information related to blockchain & digital currency projects, including interviews, podcasts, paper reviews, job listings, and more! It's one of the best resources out there if you want to learn something about blockchains or get your project reviewed by industry experts :)

PFP: This stands for printful proof and means that a non-fungible token is created & owned by a user who distributes it.

Rug: This happens when a drop team "pulls the rug out" on a project. Perhaps they had promised all sorts of extraordinary developments, activities, and community benefits after the ETH dropped, but then they simply scooped up the ETH and ran away with it. That'd be a rug. The project was toughened. You've been toughened up. Not ideal at all. Unfortunately prevalent practice

Troll: This is a buyer who offers hundreds of thousands of dollars in Ether through a buying channel like OpenSea but then never sends payment even after being informed that sellers will only accept payments from non-troll buyers :)

Smart Contract: This term describes Ethereum-based applications on the blockchain network. These are the programs that hold non-fungible tokens (NFTs) in their data storage :)

Sweep the floor: To sweep the floor is to buy NFTs at a predetermined floor price. This is frequently done by investors who believe in a project and wish to purchase extra NFTs from a set while also assisting in the rise of the floor price (because, if they and others buy up the lowest-price NFTs, the floor price naturally rises, which can positively impact the perception of value).

Whitelist: A list of people allowed to invest in a sale. They go through KYC & AML procedures before investing.

Wallet: A wallet is an account owned by someone who stores their NFTs or other cryptocurrencies. It also generally contains two cryptographically linked private keys - one being the address used for transferring tokens and another being a password known only to its owner.

CONCLUSION

Blockchain technology, cryptocurrency, and NFTs offer much potential for businesses and individuals. These technologies can create new business models and experiences that were not possible before. With the right application, they have the potential to revolutionize industries and change the way we interact with the world.

However, it is essential to remember that these technologies are still in their early stages of development. There is much uncertainty surrounding them, and their future applications are still being explored. As such, it is essential to approach them cautiously and understand the risks before investing money into them.

I hope this book has helped you to understand these technologies and their potential applications better.

9 789356 281721

Printed by Libri Plureos GmbH in Hamburg,
Germany